NONE
DARE CALL IT
CONSPIRACY

BOOKS BY GARY ALLEN

Communist Revolution in the Streets
Richard Nixon: The Man Behind the Mask
Nixon's Palace Guard
None Dare Call It Conspiracy
The Rockefeller File
Kissinger: The Secret Side of the Secretary of State
Jimmy Carter/Jimmy Carter
Ted Kennedy: In Over His Head

GARY ALLEN and LARRY ABRAHAM

NONE
DARE CALL IT
CONSPIRACY

Buccaneer Books
Cutchogue, New York

ISBN: 0899666612
ISBN-13: 97808996617

For ordering information, contact:

Buccaneer Books, Inc.
P.O. Box 168
Cutchogue, N.Y. 11935

(631) 734-5724, Fax (631) 734-7920
    www.BuccaneerBooks.com

TABLE OF CONTENTS

INTRODUCTION

It was an incredible sight. Four tractor-trailors, each looking a block long, were coming down the suburban side street to our warehouse.

Each 18-wheeler contained over 250,000 copies of *None Dare Call It Conspiracy*, a new book by Gary Allen and Larry Abraham. Over *one million copies* of a book that had only been on the market for a couple of months were being delivered — and so great was the demand that there would not be time to stack the cartons in the warehouse!

By the time the trucks were ready to unload, a gang of workers was in place. As boxes came down the conveyor belt from the truck, one person grabbed the carton and set it aside; another slapped a shipping label on it; a third affixed the proper postage; a fourth checked off the order, making sure the correct number of cartons was ready to be mailed.

For weeks orders for *None Dare Call It Conspiracy* had poured into the American Opinion Wholesale Book Division. The first printing of 250,000 books had been sold out in a matter of days. By the time the second printing was completed, we had received orders for almost one million copies.

For a couple of days, the scene in the parking lot resembled a colony of ants attacking a picnic. But instead of drumsticks and cupcakes, the targets were cartons of books.

By the end of the second day, all four tractor-trailers had been unloaded. Every advance order had been filled; every box had the proper postage and label put on it; and, nearly one million books were on their way to waiting customers — customers who began distributing copies by the hundreds, then by the thousands, to friends, neighbors, voters, and business acquaintances.

None Dare Call It Conspiracy exploded onto the political scene in March 1972. The first edition was a small paperbound book, just 144 pages long, with a cover price of $1.00. A sliding scale had been established to encourage quantity orders; for purchases of 1,000 or more copies, the cost was just 25 cents each. (That was in the days before the Nixon-Ford-Carter inflation. In the past decade, paper, printing, and production costs have sky-rocketed so high that such a price structure is now impossible.)

Less than a year after publication, concerned Americans had purchased and distributed *over 4 million copies* of this powerful little paperbound book — all without the benefit of a national advertising campaign, standard bookstore and newsstand distribution, reviews in the major media, or any other "normal" form of book promotion.

None Dare Call It Conspiracy became the fastest-selling book in publishing history for one very simple reason: Readers were fascinated by the story it told, and they bought multiple copies so *their* friends would read it.

The *Introduction* to the original printing promised that, "After reading this book, you will never look at national and world events in the same way again." For the first time, the average American could study a small, easy-to-read book, which proved through simple explanations and thorough documentation that there *was* purpose and planning behind national and international events. They could read for themselves the statements and actions of many conspirators. And by the millions, readers came away convinced that a self-perpetuating conspiracy of elitists *did* exist, with its members drawn from the highest levels of government, banking, business, education, the mass media, and more.

That conspiracy of internationalist manipulators is still in place today. Its members continue to dominate the highest councils of our government — regardless of whether a "liberal" Democrat or a "conservative" Republican occupies the White House. These elitists occupy the most powerful positions in banking, network television, important magazines and newspapers, tax-free foundations, and more. They seek the same things today that they did eleven years ago: centralized power, planned economies, and redistribution of the wealth (with themselves doing the redistributing). These are the men (and women) responsible for the warfare/welfare mentality that has dominated the West for over forty years. They have subsidized the industrialization of the Soviet Union (with *our* taxes and *our* technology), and now they are doing the same thing with Communist China. They have led our nation into two "no-win" wars in Korea and Vietnam, plus scores of lesser "brush-fires" around the world.

There are some who contend that all the failures, setbacks, and defeats for freedom in the past fifty years are simply the result of "accident." They blame poor planning, faulty execution, weak intelligence—or, in some cases, they credit an almost invincible enemy.

None of these is true.

As Gary Allen and Larry Abraham show so effectively in the pages that follow, a small group of "Insiders" have known all along *exactly* what they were doing. While this expose reads like a best-selling spy novel, *every word of it is fact*. As the authors said in the original edition, "Read it...and judge for yourself."

None Dare Call It Conspiracy is being reissued now, more than ten years after the original publication, for several reasons. We hope that people who read it a decade ago will *read it again*, and judge its contents by what has happened in the intervening decade.

If you have never read *None Dare Call It Conspiracy* before, a note of caution: you will be shocked, dismayed, angered, and perhaps horrified by what follows. But you will also understand, perhaps for the first time, why freedom seems to be on the defensive, almost always and everywhere.

Finally, after reading *None Dare Call It Conspiracy* now, you will be better prepared for two new publications by the same authors:

● *Insider Report,* the private monthly intelligence newsletter by Gary Allen and Larry Abraham. It will continue the story they told in these pages; even more important, it will tell you how you can protect yourself *and profit* from what they have learned. (For a sample copy, please use the coupon that appears on the inside back cover of this book.)

● *Now Call It Conspiracy,* a sequel to this bombshell publication. Scheduled for release in late 1983, *Now Call It Conspiracy* will detail what the "Insiders" have been doing for the past eleven years — and how they can still be exposed and defeated.

Gary Allen and Larry Abraham, in the pages that follow, show that the decline of the West is no accident.

But even more important, they prove that *freedom* and *financial prosperity* are inextricably linked together; one cannot exist without the other.

It is to protect the former, and advance the latter, that this publication is being released once again. We hope you find it of great benefit in planning and providing for your own future.

Wallis W. Wood

Chapter I

Don't Confuse Me With Facts

M OST OF us have had the experience, either as parents or youngsters, of trying to discover the "hidden picture" within another picture in a children's magazine. Usually you are shown a landscape with trees, bushes, flowers and other bits of nature. The caption reads something like this: "Concealed somewhere in this picture is a donkey pulling a cart with a boy in it. Can you find them?" Try as you might, usually you could not find the hidden picture until you turned to a page farther back in the magazine which would reveal how cleverly the artist had hidden it from us. If we study the landscape we realize that the whole picture was painted in such a way as to conceal the real picture within, and once we see the "real picture," it stands out like the proverbial painful digit.

We believe the picture painters of the mass media are artfully creating landscapes for us which deliberately hide the real picture. In this book we will show you how to discover the "hidden picture" in the landscapes presented to us daily through newspapers, radio and television. Once you can see through the camouflage, you will see the donkey, the cart and the boy who have been there all along.

9

Millions of Americans are concerned and frustrated over mishappenings in our nation. They feel that something is wrong, drastically wrong, but because of the picture painters they can't quite put their fingers on it.

Maybe you are one of those persons. Something is bugging you, but you aren't sure what. We keep electing new Presidents who seemingly promise faithfully to halt the worldwide Communist advance, put the blocks to extravagant government spending, douse the fires of inflation, put the economy on an even keel, reverse the trend which is turning the country into a moral sewer, and toss the criminals into the hoosegow where they belong. Yet, despite high hopes and glittering campaign promises, these problems continue to worsen no matter who is in office. Each new administration, whether it be Republican or Democrat, continues the same basic policies of the previous administration which it had so thoroughly denounced during the election campaign. It is considered poor form to mention this, but it is true nonetheless. Is there a plausible reason to explain why this happens? We are not supposed to think so. We are supposed to think it is all accidental and coincidental and that therefore there is nothing we can do about it.

FDR once said "In politics, nothing happens by accident. If it happens, you can bet it was planned that way." He was in a good position to know. We believe that many of the major world events that are shaping our destinies occur because somebody or somebodies have planned them that way. If we were merely dealing with the law of averages, half of the events affecting our nation's well-being should be good for America. If we were dealing with mere incompetence, our leaders should occasionally make a mistake in our favor. We shall attempt to prove that we are not really dealing with coincidence or stupidity, but with planning and brilliance. This small book deals with that planning and brilliance and how it has shaped the foreign and domestic policies of the last six administrations. We hope it will explain matters which have up to now seemed inexplicable; that it will bring into sharp focus images which have been obscured by the landscape painters of the mass media.

Those who believe that major world events result from planning are laughed at for believing in the "conspiracy theory of history." Of course, no one in this modern day and age really believes in the conspiracy theory of history —except those who have taken the time to study the subject. When you think about it, there are really only two theories of history. Either things happen by accident neither planned nor caused by anybody, or they happen because they *are* planned and somebody causes them to happen. In reality, it is the "accidental theory of history" preached in the unhallowed Halls of Ivy which should be ridiculed. Otherwise, why does every recent administration make the same mistakes as the previous ones? Why do they repeat the errors of the past which produce inflation, depression and war? Why does our State Department "stumble" from one Communist-aiding "blunder" to another? If you believe it is all an accident or the result of mysterious and unexplainable tides of history, you will be regarded as an "intellectual" who understands that we live in a complex world. If you believe that something like 32,496 consecutive coincidences over the past forty years stretches the law of averages a bit, you are a kook!

Why is it that virtually all "reputable" scholars and mass media columnists and commentators reject the cause and effect or conspiratorial theory of history? Primarily, most scholars follow the crowd in the academic world just as most women follow fashions. To buck the tide means social and professional ostracism. The same is true of the mass media. While professors and pontificators profess to be tolerant and broadminded, in practice it's strictly a one way street—with all traffic flowing left. A Maoist can be tolerated by Liberals of Ivory Towerland or by the Establishment's media pundits, but to be a conservative, and a conservative who propounds a conspiratorial view, is absolutely *verboten*. Better you should be a drunk at a national WCTU convention!

Secondly, these people have over the years acquired a strong vested emotional interest in their own errors. Their intellects and egos are totally committed to the accidental theory. Most people are highly reluctant to admit that they have been conned or have shown poor judgment. To inspect the evidence of the existence of a conspiracy guiding our political destiny from behind the scenes would force many of these people to repudiate a lifetime of accumulated opinions. It takes a person with strong character indeed to face the facts and admit he has been wrong even if it was because he was uninformed.

Such was the case with the author of this book. It was only because he set out to prove the conservative anti-Communists wrong that he happened to end up writing this book. His initial reaction to the conservative point of view was one of suspicion and hostility; and it was only after many months of intensive research that he had to admit that he had been "conned."

Politicians and "intellectuals" are attracted to the concept that events are propelled by some mysterious tide of history or happen by accident. By this reasoning they hope to escape blame when things go wrong.

Most intellectuals, pseudo or otherwise, deal with the conspiratorial theory of history simply by ignoring it. They never attempt to refute the evidence. It can't be refuted. If and when the silent treatment doesn't work, these "objective" scholars and mass media opinion molders resort to personal attacks, ridicule and satire. The personal attacks tend to divert attention from the facts which an author or speaker is trying to expose. The idea is to force the person exposing the conspiracy to stop the exposure and spend his time and effort defending himself.

However, the most effective weapons used against the conspiratorial theory of history are ridicule and satire. These extremely potent weapons can be cleverly used to avoid any honest attempt at refuting the facts. After all, nobody likes to be made fun of. Rather than be ridiculed most people will keep quiet; and, this subject certainly does lend itself to ridicule and satire. One technique which can be used is to expand the conspiracy to the extent it becomes absurd. For instance, our man from the Halls of Poison Ivy might say in a scoffingly arrogant tone, "I suppose you believe every liberal professor gets a telegram each morning from conspiracy head-quarters containing his orders for the day's brainwashing of his students?" Some conspiratorialists do indeed overdraw the picture by expanding the conspiracy (from the small clique which it is) to include every local knee-jerk liberal activist and government bureaucrat. Or, because of racial or religious bigotry, they will take small fragments of legitimate evidence and expand them into a conclusion that will support their particular prejudice, i.e., the conspiracy is totally "Jewish," "Catholic," or "Masonic." These people do not help to expose the conspiracy, but, sadly play into the hands of those who want the public to believe that all conspiratorialsts are screwballs.

"Intellectuals" are fond of mouthing cliches like "The conspiracy theory is often tempting. However, it is overly simplistic." To ascribe absolutely everything that happens to the machinations of a small group of power hungry conspirators *is* overly simplistic. But, in our opinion nothing is more simplistic than doggedly holding onto the accidental view of major world events.

In most cases Liberals simply accuse all those who discuss the conspiracy of being paranoid. "Ah, you right wingers," they say, "rustling every bush, kicking over every rock, looking for imaginary boogeymen." Then comes the *coup de grace* —labeling the conspiratorial theory as the "devil theory of history." The Liberals love that one. Even though it is an empty phrase, it sounds so sophisticated!

With the leaders of the academic and communications

world assuming this sneering attitude towards the conspiratorial (or cause and effect) theory of history, it is not surprising that millions of innocent and well-meaning people, in a natural desire not to appear naive, assume the attitudes and repeat the cliches of the opinion makers. These persons, in their attempt to appear sophisticated, assume their mentors' air of smug superiority even though they themselves have not spent five minutes in study on the subject of international conspiracy.

The "accidentalists" would have us believe that ascribing any of our problems to planning is "simplistic" and all our problems are caused by Poverty, Ignorance and Disease—hereinafter abbreviated as PID. They ignore the fact that organized conspirators use PID, real and imagined, as an excuse to build a jail for us all. Most of the world has been in PID since time immemorial and it takes incredibly superficial thinking to ascribe the ricocheting of the United States government from one disaster to another over the past thirty years to PID. "Accidentalists" ignore the fact that some of the more advanced nations in the world have been captured by Communists. Czechoslovakia was one of the world's most modern industrial nations and Cuba had the second highest per capita income of any nation in Central and South America.

It is not true, however, to state that there are no members of the intellectual elite who subscribe to the conspiratorial theory of history. For example, there is Professor Carroll Quigley of the Foreign Service School at Georgetown University. Professor Quigley can hardly be accused of being a "right wing extremist." (Those three words have been made inseparable by the mass media.) Dr. Quigley has all the "liberal" credentials, having taught at the Liberal Establishment's academic Meccas of Princeton and Harvard. In his 1300-page, 8 pound tome *Tragedy and Hope*, Dr. Quigley reveals the existence of the conspiratorial network which will be discussed in this book. The Professor is not merely formulating a theory, but revealing this network's existence from firsthand experience. He also makes it clear that it is only the network's secrecy and not their goals to which he objects. Professor Quigley discloses:

> "I know the operations of this network because I have studied it for twenty years and was permitted for two years, in the early 1960's, to examine its papers and secret records. I HAVE NO AVERSION TO IT OR TO MOST OF ITS AIMS AND HAVE, FOR MUCH OF MY LIFE, BEEN CLOSE TO IT AND TO MANY OF ITS INSTRUMENTS. I have objected, both in the past and recently, to a few of its policies . . . but in general my chief difference of opinion is that IT WISHES TO REMAIN UNKNOWN, and I believe its role in history is significant enough to be known." (p. 950 emphasis added)

We agree, its role in history does deserve to be known. That is why we have written this book. However, we most emphatically disagree with this network's aim which the Professor describes as "nothing less than to create a world system of financial control in private hands able to dominate the political system of each country and the economy of the world as a whole." In other words, this power mad clique wants to control and rule the world. Even more frightening, they want total control over all individual actions. As Professor Quigley observes: ". . . his [the individual's] freedom and choice will be controlled within very narrow alternatives by the fact that he will be numbered from birth and followed, as a number, through his educational training, his required military or other public service, his tax contributions, his health and medical requirements, and his final retirement and death benefits." It wants control over all natural resources, business, banking and transportation by controlling the governments of the world. In order to accomplish these aims the

15

conspirators have had no qualms about fomenting wars, depressions and hatred. They want a monopoly which would eliminate all competitors and destroy the free enterprise system. And Professor Quigley, of Harvard, Princeton and Georgetown *approves!*

Professor Quigley is not the only academic who is aware of the existence of a clique of self-perpetuating conspirators whom we shall call *Insiders*. Other honest scholars finding the same individuals at the scenes of disastrous political fires over and over again have concluded that there is obviously an organization of pyromaniacs at work in the world. But these intellectually honest scholars realize that if they challenged the *Insiders* head-on, their careers would be destroyed. The author knows these men exist because he has been in contact with some of them.

There are also religious leaders who are aware of the existence of this conspiracy. In a UPI story dated December 27, 1965, Father Pedro Arrupe, head of the Jesuit Order of the Roman Catholic Church, made the following charges during his remarks to the Ecumenical Council:

> This . . . Godless society operates in an extremely efficient manner at least in its higher levels of leadership. It makes use of every possible means at its disposal, be they scientific, technical, social or economic.
> It follows a perfectly mapped-out strategy. It holds almost complete sway in international organizations, in financial circles, in the field of mass communications; press, cinema, radio and television."

There are a number of problems to be overcome in convincing a person of the possible existence of a conspiratorial clique of *Insiders* who from the very highest levels manipulate government policy. In this case truth is really stranger than fiction. We are dealing with history's greatest "whodunit," a

16

mystery thriller which puts Erle Stanley Gardner to shame. If you love a mystery, you'll be fascinated with the study of the operations of the *Insiders*. If you do study this network of which Professor Quigley speaks, you will find that what had at first seemed incredible not only exists, but heavily influences our lives.

It must be remembered that the first job of any conspiracy, whether it be in politics, crime or within a business office, is to convince everyone else that no conspiracy exists. The conspirators' success will be determined largely by their ability to do this. That the elite of the academic world and mass communications media always pooh-pooh the existence of the *Insiders* merely serves to camouflage their operations. These "artists" hide the boy, the cart and the donkey.

Probably at some time you have been involved with or had personal knowledge of some event which was reported in the news. Perhaps it concerned an athletic event, an election, a committee or your business. Did the report contain the "real" story, the story behind the story? Probably not. And for a variety of reasons. The reporter had time and space problems and there is a good chance the persons involved deliberately did not reveal all the facts. Possibly the reporter's own prejudices governed what facts went into the story and which were deleted. Our point is that most people know from personal experience that a news story often is not the whole story. But many of us assume that our own case is unique when really it is typical. What is true about the reporting of local events is equally as true about the reporting of national and international events.

Psychological problems are also involved in inducing people to look at the evidence concerning the *Insiders*. People are usually comfortable with their old beliefs and conceptions. When Columbus told people the world was a ball and not a pancake, they were highly upset. They were being asked to reject their way of thinking of a lifetime and adopt a whole new outlook. The "intellectuals" of the day scoffed at Columbus and people were afraid they would lose social prestige if they listened to him. Many others just did not want to believe the world was round. It complicated too many things. And typical flat-earthers had such a vested interest involving their own egos, that they heaped abuse on Columbus for challenging their view of the universe. "Don't confuse us with facts; our minds are made up," they said.

These same factors apply today. Because the Establishment controls the media, anyone exposing the *Insiders* will be the recipient of a continuous fusillade of invective from newspapers, magazines, TV and radio. In this manner one is threatened with loss of "social respectability" if he dares broach the idea that there is organization behind any of the problems currently wracking America. Unfortunately, for many people social status comes before intellectual honesty. Although they would never admit it, social position is more important to many people than is the survival of freedom in America.

If you ask these people which is more important—social respectability or saving their children from slavery—they will tell you the latter, of course. But their actions (or lack of same) speak so much louder than their words. People have an infinite capacity for rationalization when it comes to refusing to face the threat to America's survival. Deep down these people are afraid they may be laughed at if they take a stand, or may be denied an invitation to some social climber's cocktail party. Instead of getting mad at the *Insiders*, these people actually get angry at those who are trying to save the country by exposing the conspirators.

One thing which makes it so hard for some socially minded people to assess the conspiratorial evidence objectively is that the conspirators come from the very highest social strata. They are immensely wealthy, highly educated and extremely cultured. Many of them have lifelong reputations for philanthropy. Nobody enjoys being put in the position of accusing prominent people of conspiring to enslave their fellow Americans, but the facts are inescapable. Many business and professional people are particularly vulnerable to the "don't jeopardize your social respectability" pitch given by those who don't want the conspiracy exposed. The *Insiders* know that if the business and professional community will not take a stand to save the private enterprise system, the socialism through which they intend to control the world will be inevitable. They believe that most business and professional men are too shallow and decadent, too status conscious, too tied up in the problems of their jobs and businesses to worry about what is going on in politics. These men are told that it might be bad for business or jeopardize their government contracts if they take a stand. They have been bribed into silence with their own tax monies!

We are hoping that the conspirators have underestimated the courage and patriotism remaining in the American people. We feel there are a sufficient number of you who are not mesmerized by the television set, who put God, family and country above social status, who will band together to expose and destroy the conspiracy of the *Insiders*. The philosopher Diogenes scoured the length and breadth of ancient Greece searching for an honest man. We are scouring the length and breadth of America in search of hundreds of thousands of intellectually honest men and women who are willing to investigate facts and come to logical conclusions—no matter how unpleasant those conclusions may be.

Chapter II

Socialism—Royal Road to Power for the Super-Rich

E VERYONE knows that Adolph Hitler existed. No one disputes that. The terror and destruction that this madman inflicted upon the world are universally recognized. Hitler came from a poor family which had absolutely no social position. He was a high school drop-out and nobody ever accused him of being cultured. Yet this man tried to conquer the world. During his early career he sat in a cold garret and poured onto paper his ambitions to rule the world. We know that.

Similarly, we know that a man named Vladimir Ilich Lenin also existed. Like Hitler, Lenin did not spring from a family of social lions. The son of a petty bureaucrat, Lenin, who spent most of his adult life in poverty, has been responsible for the deaths of tens of millions of your fellow human beings and the enslavement of nearly a billion more. Like Hitler, Lenin sat up nights in a dank garret scheming how he could conquer the world. We know that too.

Is it not theoretically possible that a billionaire could be sitting, not in a garret, but in a penthouse, in Manhattan, London or Paris and dream the same dream as Lenin and Hitler? You will have to admit it is theoretically possible. Julius Caesar, a wealthy aristocrat, did. And such a man might form an alliance or association with other like-minded men, might he not? Caesar did. These men would be superbly educated, command immense social prestige and be able to pool astonishing amounts of money to carry out their purposes. These are advantages that Hitler and Lenin did not have.

It is difficult for the average individual to fathom such perverted lust for power. The typical person, of whatever nationality, wants only to enjoy success in his job, to be able to afford a reasonably high standard of living complete with leisure and travel. He wants to provide for his family in sickness and in health and to give his children a sound education. His ambition stops there. He has no desire to exercise power over others, to conquer other lands or peoples, to be a king. He wants to mind his own business and enjoy life. Since he has no lust for power, it is difficult for him to imagine that there are others who have . . . others who march to a far different drum. But we must realize that there *have* been Hitlers and Lenins and Stalins and Caesars and Alexander the Greats throughout history. Why should we assume there are no such men today with perverted lusts for power? And if these men happen to be billionaires is it not possible that they would use men like Hitler and Lenin as pawns to seize power for themselves?

Indeed, difficult as this is to believe, such is the case. Like Columbus, we are faced with the task of convincing you that the world is not flat, as you have been led to believe all your life, but, instead, is round. We are going to present evidence that what you call "Communism" is not run from Moscow or Peking, but is an arm of a bigger conspiracy run from New York, London and Paris. The men at the apex of this movement are not Communists in the traditional sense of that term. They feel no loyalty to Moscow or Peking. They are loyal only to themselves and their undertaking. And these men certainly do not believe in the clap-trap pseudo-philosophy of Communism. They have no intention of dividing their wealth. Socialism is a philosophy which conspirators exploit, but in

22

which only the naive believe. Just how finance capitalism is used as the anvil and Communism as the hammer to conquer the world will be explained in this book.

The concept that Communism is but an arm of a larger conspiracy has become increasingly apparent throughout the author's journalistic investigations. He has had the opportunity to interview privately four retired officers who spent their careers high in military intelligence. Much of what the author knows he learned from them. And the story is known to several thousand others. High military intelligence circles are well aware of this network. In addition, the author has interviewed six men who have spent considerable time as investigators for Congressional committees. In 1953, one of these men, Norman Dodd, headed the Reece Committee's investigation of tax-free foundations. When Mr. Dodd began delving into the role of international high finance in the world revolutionary movement, the investigation was killed on orders from the Eisenhower-occupied White House. According to Mr. Dodd, it is permissible to investigate the radical bomb throwers in the streets, but when you begin to trace their activities back to their origins in the "legitimate world," the political iron curtain slams down.

You can believe anything you want about Communism except that it is a conspiracy run by men from the respectable world. People will often say to an active anti-Communist: "I can understand your concern with Communism, but the idea that a Communist conspiracy is making great inroads in the United States is absurd. The American people are anti-Communist. They're not about to buy Communism. It's understandable to be concerned about Communism in Africa or Asia or South America with their tremendous poverty, ignorance and disease. But to be concerned about Communism in the United States where the vast majority of people have no sympathy with it whatsoever is a misspent concern."

On the face of it, that is a very logical and plausible argument. The American people are indeed anti-Communist. Suppose you were to lay this book down right now, pick up a clip board and head for the nearest shopping center to conduct a survey on Americans' attitudes about Communism. "Sir," you say to the first prospect you encounter, "we would like to know if you are for or against Communism?"

Most people would probably think you were putting them on. If we stick to our survey we would find that ninety-nine percent of the people are anti-Communist. We probably would be hard put to find anybody who would take an affirmative stand for Communism.

So, on the surface it appears that the charges made against anti-Communists concerned with the internal threat of Communism are valid. The American people are not pro-Communist. But before our imaginary interviewee walks away in disgust with what he believes is a hokey survey, you add: "Sir, before you leave there are a couple of other questions I would like to ask. You won't find these quite so insulting or ludicrous." Your next question is: "What is Communism? Will you define it, please?"

Immediately a whole new situation has developed. Rather than the near unanimity previously found, we now have an incredible diversity of ideas. There are a multitude of opinions on what Communism is. Some will say: "Oh, yes, Communism. Well, that's a tyrannical brand of socialism." Others will maintain: "Communism as it was originally intended by Karl Marx was a good idea. But it has never been practiced and the Russians have loused it up." A more erudite type might proclaim: "Communism is simply a rebirth of Russian imperialism."

If perchance one of the men you ask to define Communism happened to be a political science professor from the local college, he might well reply: "You can't ask 'what is Communism?' That is a totally simplistic question about an extremely complex situation. Communism today, quite unlike the view held by the right wing extremists in America, is not an international monolithic movement. Rather, it is a polycentric, fragmented, nationalistic movement deriving its character through the charisms of its various national leaders. While, of course, there is the welding of Hegelian dialects with Feuerbachian materialism held in common by the Communist parties generally, it is a monumental oversimplification to ask 'what is Communism.' Instead you should ask: What is the Communism of Mao Tse-tung? What is the Communism of the late Ho Chi Minh, or Fidel Castro or Marshal Tito?"

If you think we are being facetious here, you haven't talked to a political science professor lately. For the above is the prevailing view on our campuses, not to mention in our State Department.

Whether you agree or disagree with any of these definitions, or, as may well be the case, you have one of your own, one thing is undeniable. No appreciable segment of the anti-Communist American public can agree on just what it is that they are against. Isn't that frightening? Here we have something that almost everybody agrees is bad, but we cannot agree on just what it is we are against.

How would this work in a football game, for example? Can you imagine how effective the defense of a football team would be if the front four could not agree with the linebackers who could not agree with the corner backs who could not agree with the safety men who could not agree with the assistant coaches who could not agree with the head coach as to what kind of defense they should put up against the offense being presented? The obvious result would be chaos. You could take a sand lot team and successfully pit them against the Green Bay Packers if the Packers couldn't agree on what it is they are opposing. This is academic. The first principle in any encounter, whether it be football or war (hot or cold), is: Know your enemy. Consequently, it is not strange at all that for three decades we have been watching one country of the world after another fall behind the Communist curtain.

In keeping with the fact that almost everybody seems to have his own definition of Communism, we are going to give you ours, and then we will attempt to prove to you that it is the only valid one. Communism: AN INTERNATIONAL, CONSPIRATORIAL DRIVE FOR POWER ON THE PART OF MEN IN HIGH PLACES WILLING TO USE ANY MEANS TO BRING ABOUT THEIR DESIRED AIM—GLOBAL CONQUEST.

You will notice that we did not mention Marx, Engels, Lenin, Trotsky, bourgeois, proletariat or dialectical materialism. We said nothing of the pseudo-economics or political philosophy of the Communists. These are the TECHNIQUES of Communism and should not be confused with the Communist conspiracy itself. We did call it an international conspiratorial drive for power. Unless we understand the conspiratorial nature of Communism, we don't understand it at all. We will be eternally fixated at the Gus Hall level of Communism. And that's not where it's at, baby!

The way to bring down the wrath of the Liberal press Establishment or the professional Liberals is simply to use the word *conspiracy* in relation to Communism. We are not supposed to believe that Communism is a political conspiracy. We can believe anything else we wish to about it. We can believe that it is brutal, tyrannical, evil or even that it intends to bury us, and we will win the plaudits of the vast majority of American people. But don't ever, ever use the word *conspiracy* if you expect applause, for that is when the wrath of Liberaldom will be unleashed against you. We are not disallowed from believing in *all* types of conspiracy, just modern political conspiracy.

We know that down through the annals of history small groups of men have existed who have conspired to bring the reins of power into their hands. History books are full of their schemes. Even *Life* magazine believes in conspiracies like the Cosa Nostra where men conspire to make money through crime. You may recall that *Life* did a series of articles on the testimony of Joseph Valachi before the McClellan Committee several years ago. There are some aspects of those revelations which are worth noting.

Most of us did not know the organization was called Cosa Nostra. Until Valachi "sang" we all thought it was named the Mafia. That is how little we knew about this group, despite the fact that it was a century old and had been operating in many countries with a self-perpetuating clique of leaders. We didn't even know it by its proper name. Is it not possible a political conspiracy might exist, waiting for a Joseph Valachi to testify? Is Dr. Carroll Quigley the Joseph Valachi of political conspiracies?

We see that everybody, even *Life* magazine, believes in some sort of conspiracy. The question is: Which is the more lethal form of conspiracy—criminal or political? And what is the difference between a member of the Cosa Nostra and a Communist, or more properly, an *Insider* conspirator? Men like Lucky Luciano who have scratched and clawed to the top of the heap in organized crime must, of necessity, be diabolically brilliant, cunning and absolutely ruthless. But, almost without exception, the men in the hierarchy of organized crime have had no formal education. They were born into poverty and learned their trade in the back alleys of Naples, New York or Chicago.

Now suppose someone with this same amoral grasping personality were born into a patrician family of great wealth and was educated at the best prep schools, then Harvard, Yale or Princeton, followed by graduate work possibly at Oxford. In these institutions he would become totally familiar with history, economics, psychology, sociology and political science. After having graduated from such illustrious establishments of higher learning, are we likely to find him out on the streets peddling fifty cent tickets to a numbers game? Would you find him pushing marijuana to high schoolers or running a string of houses of prostitution? Would he be getting involved in gangland killings? Not at all. For with that sort of education, this person would realize that if one wants power, real power, the lessons of history say, "Get into the government business." Become a politician and work for political power or, better yet, get some politicians to front for you. That is where the real power—and the real money—is.

Conspiracy to seize the power of government is as old as government itself. We can study the conspiracies surrounding Alcibiades in Greece or Julius Caesar in ancient Rome, but we are not supposed to think that men today scheme to achieve political power.

Every conspirator has two things in common with every other conspirator. He must be an accomplished liar and a far-seeing planner. Whether you are studying Hitler, Alcibiades, Julius Caesar or some of our contemporary conspirators, you will find that their patient planning is almost overwhelming. We repeat FDR's statement: "In politics, nothing happens by accident. If it happens, you can bet it was planned that way."

In reality, Communism is a tyranny planned by power seekers whose most effective weapon is the big lie. And if one takes all of the lies of Communism and boils them down, you will find they distill into two major lies out of which all others spring. They are: (1) Communism is inevitable, and (2) Communism is a movement of the downtrodden masses rising up against exploiting bosses.

Let us go back to our imaginary survey and analyze our first big lie of Communism—that it is inevitable. You will recall that we asked our interviewee if he was for or against Communism and then we asked him to define it. Now we are going to ask him: "Sir, do you think Communism is inevitable in America?" And in almost every case the response will be something like this: "Oh, well, no. I don't think so. You know how Americans are. We are a little slow sometimes in reacting to danger. You remember Pearl Harbor. But the American people would never sit still for Communism."

Next we ask: "Well then, do you think socialism is inevitable in America?" The answer, in almost every case will be similar to this: "I'm no socialist, you understand, but I see what is going on in this country. Yeah, I'd have to say that socialism is inevitable."

Then we ask our interviewee: "Since you say you are not a socialist but you feel the country is being socialized, why don't you do something about it?" His response will run: "I'm only one person. Besides it's inevitable. You can't fight city hall, heh, heh, heh."

Don't you know that the boys down at city hall are doing everything they can to convince you of that? How effectively can you oppose anything if you feel your opposition is futile? Giving your opponent the idea that defending himself is futile is as old as warfare itself. In about 500 B. C. the Chinese war lord-philosopher Sun Tsu stated, "Supreme excellence in warfare lies in the destruction of your enemy's will to resist in advance of perceptible hostilities." We call it "psy war" or psychological warfare today. In poker, it is called "running a good bluff." The principle is the same.

Thus we have the American people: anti-Communist, but unable to define it and anti-socialist, but thinking it is inevitable. How did Marx view Communism? How important is "the inevitability of Communism" to the Communists? What do the Communists want you to believe is inevitable—Communism or socialism? If you study Marx' *Communist Manifesto* you will find that in essence Marx said the proletarian revolution would establish the SOCIALIST dictatorship of the proletariat. To achieve the SOCIALIST dictatorship of the proletariat, three things would have to be accomplished: (1) The elimination of all right to private property; (2) The dissolution of the family unit; and (3) Destruction of what Marx referred to as the "opiate of the people," religion.

Marx went on to state that when the dictatorship of the proletariat had accomplished these three things throughout the world, and after some undetermined length of time (as you can imagine, he was very vague on this point), the all powerful state would miraculously wither away and state socialism would give way to Communism. You wouldn't need any government at all. Everything would be peace, sweetness and light and everybody would live happily ever after. But first, all Communists must work to establish SOCIALISM.

Can't you just see Karl Marx really believing that an omnipotent state would wither away? Or can you imagine that a Joseph Stalin (or any other man with the cunning and ruthlessness necessary to rise to the top of the heap in an all-powerful dictatorship) would voluntarily dismantle the power he had built by fear and terror?*

Socialism would be the bait . . . the excuse to establish the dictatorship. Since dictatorship is hard to sell in idealistic terms, the idea had to be added that the dictatorship was just a temporary necessity and would soon dissolve of its own accord. You really have to be naive to swallow that, but millions do!

The drive to establish SOCIALISM, not Communism, is at the core of everything the Communists and the *Insiders* do. Marx and all of his successors in the Communist movement have ordered their followers to work on building SOCIALISM. If you go to hear an official Communist speaker, he never mentions Communism. He will speak only of the struggle to complete the socialization of America. If you go to a Communist bookstore you will find that all of their literature pushes this theme. It does *not* call for the establishment of Communism, but SOCIALISM.

And many members of the Establishment push this same theme. The September 1970 issue of *New York* magazine contains an article by Harvard Professor John Kenneth Galbraith, himself a professed socialist, entitled "Richard Nixon and the

---

(*Karl Marx was hired by a mysterious group who called themselves the League of Just Men to write the *Communist Manifesto* as demogogic boob-bait to appeal to the mob. In actual fact the *Communist Manifesto* was in circulation for many years before Marx' name was widely enough recognized to establish his authorship for this revolutionary handbook. All Karl Marx really did was to update and codify the very same revolutionary plans and principles set down seventy years earlier by Adam Weishaupt, the founder of the Order of Illuminati in Bavaria. And, it is widely acknowledged by serious scholars of this subject that the League of Just Men was simply an extension of the Illuminati which was forced to go deep underground after it was exposed by a raid in 1786 conducted by the Bavarian authorities.)

Great Socialist Revival." In describing what he calls the "Nixon Game Plan," Galbraith states:

"Mr. Nixon is probably not a great reader of Marx, but [his advisors] Drs. Burns, Shultz and McCracken are excellent scholars who know him well and could have brought the President abreast and it is beyond denying that the crisis that aided the rush into socialism was engineered by the Administration. . . ."

"Certainly the least predicted development under the Nixon Administration was this great new thrust to socialism. One encounters people who still aren't aware of it. Others must be rubbing their eyes, for certainly the portents seemed all to the contrary. As an opponent of socialism, Mr. Nixon seemed steadfast. . . ."

Galbraith then proceeds to list the giant steps toward socialism taken by the Nixon Administration. The conclusion one draws from the article is that socialism, whether it be from the Democrat or Republican Parties, is inevitable. Fellow Harvard socialist Dr. Arthur Schlesinger has said the same thing:

"The chief liberal gains in the past generally remain on the statute books when the conservatives recover power . . . liberalism grows constantly more liberal, and by the same token, conservatism grows constantly less conservative. . . ."

Many extremely patriotic individuals have innocently fallen for the conspiracy's line. Walter Trohan, columnist emeritus for the *Chicago Tribune* of Oct. 5, 1970, and one of America's outstanding political commentators, has accurately noted:

"It is a known fact that the policies of the government today, whether Republican or Democratic, are closer to the 1932 platform of the Communist Party than they are to either of their own party platforms in that critical year. More than 100 years ago, in 1848 to be exact, Karl Marx promulgated his program for the socialized state in the Communist Manifesto. . . ."

And Mr. Trohan has also been led to believe that the trend is inevitable:

"Conservatives should be realistic enough to recognize that this country is going deeper into socialism and will see expansion of federal power, whether Republicans or Democrats are in power. The only comfort they may have is that the pace will be slower under Richard M. Nixon than it might have been under Hubert H. Humphrey. . . .

Conservatives are going to have to recognize that the Nixon Administration will embrace most of the socialism of the Democratic administrations, while professing to improve it. . . ." (Chi. Trib. Oct. 15, '69)

The Establishment promotes the idea of the inevitability of Communism through its perversion of terms used in describing the political spectrum. (See Chart 1) We are told that on the far Left of the political spectrum we find Communism, which is admittedly dictatorial. But, we are also told that equally to be feared is the opposite of the far Left, i.e., the far Right, which is labeled Fascism. We are constantly told that we should all try to stay in the middle of the road, which is termed democracy, but by which the Establishment means Fabian (or creeping) socialism. (The fact that the middle of the road has been moving inexorably leftward for forty years is ignored.) Here is an excellent example of the use of false alternatives. We are given the choice between Communism

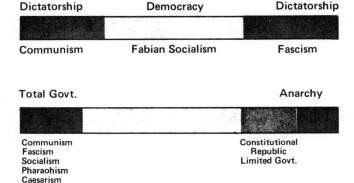

Dictatorship   Democracy   Dictatorship

Communism   Fabian Socialism   Fascism

Total Govt.   Anarchy

Communism   Constitutional
Fascism   Republic
Socialism   Limited Govt.
Pharaohism
Caesarism

Chart 1 depicts a false Left-Right political spectrum used by Liberals which has Communism (International Socialism) on the far Left and its twin, Fascism (National Socialism) on the far Right with the "middle of the road" being Fabian Socialism. The entire spectrum is Socialist!

Chart 2 is a more rational political spectrum with total government in any form on the far Left and no government or anarchy on the far right. The U. S. was a Republic with a limited government, but for the past 60 years we have been moving leftward across the spectrum towards total government with each new piece of socialist legislation.

(*international* socialism) on one end of the spectrum, Naziism (*national* socialism) on the other end, or Fabian socialism in the middle. The whole spectrum is socialist!

This is absurd. Where would you put an anarchist on this spectrum? Where do you put a person who believes in a Constitutional Republic and the free enterprise system? He is not represented here, yet this spectrum is used for political definitions by a probably ninety percent of the people of the nation.

There is an accurate political spectrum. (See Chart 2.) Communism is, by definition, total government. If you have total government it makes little difference whether you call it Communism, Fascism, Socialism, Caesarism or Pharaohism. It's all pretty much the same from the standpoint of the people who must live and suffer under it. If total government (by any of its pseudonyms) stands on the far Left, then by logic the far Right should represent anarchy, or no government.

Our Founding Fathers revolted against the near-total government of the English monarchy. But they knew that having no government at all would lead to chaos. So they set up a Constitutional Republic with a very limited government. They knew that men prospered in freedom. Although the free enterprise system is not mentioned specifically in the Constitution, it is the only one which can exist under a Constitutional Republic. All collectivist systems require power in government which the Constitution did not grant. Our Founding Fathers had no intention of allowing the government to become an instrument to steal the fruit of one man's labor and give it to another who had not earned it. Our government was to be one of severely limited powers. Thomas Jefferson said: "In questions of power then let no more be heard of confidence in man, but bind him down from mischief by the chains of the Constitution."⑥ Jefferson knew that if the government were not enslaved, people soon would be.

It was Jefferson's view that government governs best which governs least. Our forefathers established this country with the very least possible amount of government. Although they lived in an age before automobiles, electric lights and television, they understood human nature and its relation to political systems far better than do most Americans today. Times change, technology changes, but principles are eternal. Primarily, government was to provide for national defense and to establish a court system. But we have burst the chains that Jefferson spoke of and for many years now we have been moving leftward across the political spectrum toward collectivist total government. Every proposal by our political leaders¨ (including some which are supposed to have the very opposite effect, such as Nixon's revenue sharing proposal) carries us further leftward to centralized government. This is not because socialism is inevitable. It is no more inevitable than Pharaohism. It is largely the result of clever planning and patient gradualism.

Since all Communists and their *Insider* bosses are waging a constant struggle for SOCIALISM, let us define that term. Socialism is usually defined as government ownership and/or control over the basic means of production and distribution of goods and services. When analyzed this means government control over everything, including you. All controls are "people" controls. If the government controls these areas it can eventually do just exactly as Marx set out to do—destroy the right to private property, eliminate the family and wipe out religion.

We are being socialized in America and everybody knows it. If we had a chance to sit down and have a cup of coffee with the man in the street that we have been interviewing, he might say: "You know, the one thing I can never figure out is why all these very, very wealthy people like the Kennedys, the Fords, the Rockefellers and others are for socialism. Why are the super-rich for socialism? Don't they have the most to lose? I take a look at my bank account and compare it with Nelson Rockefeller's and it seems funny that I'm against socialism and he's out promoting it." Or is it funny? In reality, there is a vast difference between what the promoters define as socialism and what it is in actual practice. The idea that socialism is a share-the-wealth program is strictly a confidence game to get the people to surrender their freedom to an all-powerful collectivist government. While the *Insiders* tell us we are building a paradise on earth, we are actually constructing a jail for ourselves.

Doesn't it strike you as strange that some of the individuals pushing hardest for socialism have their own personal wealth protected in family trusts and tax-free foundations? Men like Rockefeller, Ford and Kennedy are for every socialist program known to man which will increase your taxes. Yet they pay little, if anything, in taxes themselves. An article published by the North American Newspaper Alliance in August of 1967 tells how the Rockefellers pay practically no income taxes despite their vast wealth. The article reveals that one of the Rockefellers paid the grand total of $685 personal income tax during a recent year. The Kennedys have their Chicago Merchandise Mart, their mansions, yachts, planes, etc., all owned by their myriads of family foundations and trusts. Taxes are for peons! Yet hypocrites like Rockefeller, Ford and Kennedy pose as great champions of the "downtrodden." If they were really concerned about the poor, rather than using socialism as a means of achieving personal political power, they would divest themselves of their own fortunes. There is no law which prevents them from giving away their own fortunes to the poverty stricken. Shouldn't these men set an example? And practice what they preach? If they advocate sharing the wealth, shouldn't they start with their own instead of that of the middle class which pays almost all the taxes? Why don't Nelson Rockefeller and Henry Ford II give away all their wealth, retaining only enough to place themselves at the national average? Can't you imagine Teddy Kennedy giving up his mansion, airplane and yacht and moving into a $25,000 home with a $20,000 mortgage like the rest of us?

We are usually told that this clique of super-rich are socialists because they have a guilt complex over wealth they inherited and did not earn. Again, they could relieve these supposed guilt complexes simply by divesting themselves of their unearned wealth. There are doubtless many wealthy do-gooders who have been given a guilt complex by their college professors, but that doesn't explain the actions of *Insiders* like the Rockefellers, Fords or Kennedys. All their actions betray them as power seekers.

But the Kennedys, Rockefellers and their super-rich confederates are not being hypocrites in advocating socialism. It appears to be a contradiction for the super-rich to work for socialism and the destruction of free enterprise. In reality it is not.

Our problem is that most of us believe socialism is what the socialists want us to believe it is—a share-the-wealth program. That is the theory. But is that how it works? Let us examine the only Socialist countries—according to the Socialist definition of the word—extant in the world today. These are the Communist countries. The Communists themselves refer to these as Socialist countries, as in the Union of Soviet Socialist Republics. Here in the reality of socialism you have a tiny oligarchial clique at the top, usually numbering no more than three percent of the total population, controlling the total wealth, total production and the very lives of the other ninety-seven percent. Certainly even the most naive observe that Mr. Brezhnev doesn't live like one of the poor peasants out on the great Russian steppes. But, according to socialist theory, he is supposed to do just that!

If one understands that socialism is not a share-the-wealth program, but is in reality a method to *consolidate* and *control* the wealth, then the seeming paradox of super-rich men promoting socialism becomes no paradox at all. Instead it becomes the logical, even the perfect tool of power-seeking megalomaniacs. Communism, or more accurately, socialism, is not a movement of the downtrodden masses, but of the economic elite. The plan of the conspirator *Insiders* then is to socialize the United States, not to Communize it.

How is this to be accomplished? Chart 3 shows the structure of our government as established by our Founding Fathers. The Constitution fractionalized and subdivided governmental power in every way possible. The Founding Fathers believed that each branch of the government, whether at the federal, state or local level, would be jealous of its powers and would never surrender them to centralized control. Also, many phases of our lives (such as charity and education) were put totally, or almost totally, out of the grasp of politicians. *Under this system you could not have a dictatorship.* No segment of government could possibly amass enough power to form a dictatorship. In order to have a dictatorship one must have a single branch holding most of the reins of power. Once you have this, a dictatorship is inevitable.

CONSTITUTIONAL REPUBLIC

FEDERAL GOVT.

STATE GOVTS.

Labor Finance Business Executive Legislative Judicial Courts City County Charity Police Educ.

DEMOCRATIC SOCIALISM

EXECUTIVE

Labor Finance Business Legislative Judicial States Counties Cities Charity Police Educ.

A dictatorship was impossible in our Republic because power was widely diffused. Today, as we approach Democratic Socialism, all power is being centralized at the apex of the executive branch of the federal government. This concentration of power makes a dictatorship inevitable. Those who control the President indirectly gain virtual control of the whole country.

The English philosopher Thomas Hobbes noted: "Freedom is government divided into small fragments." Woodrow Wilson, before he became the tool of the *Insiders,* observed: "This history of liberty is a history of the limitations of governmental power, not the increase of it." And the English historian Lord Acton commented: "Power tends to corrupt and absolute power corrupts absolutely." Even though these men lived after our Constitution was written, our forefathers understood these principles completely.

But what is happening today? As we move leftward along the political spectrum towards socialism, all the reins of power are being centralized in the executive branch of the federal government. Much of this is being done by buying with legislation or with "free" federal grants all the other entities. Money is used as bait and the hook is federal control. The Supreme Court has ruled, and in this case quite logically, that "it is hardly lack of due process for the government to regulate that which it subsidizes."

If you and your clique wanted control over the United States, it would be impossible to take over every city hall, county seat and state house. You would want all power vested at the apex of the executive branch of the federal government; then you would have only to control one man to control the whole shebang. If you wanted to control the nation's manufacturing, commerce, finance, transportation and natural resources, you would need only to control the apex, the power pinnacle, of an all-powerful SOCIALIST government. Then you would have a monopoly and could squeeze out all your competitors. If you wanted a national monopoly, you must control a national socialist government. If you want a worldwide monopoly, you must control a world socialist government. That is what the game is all about. "Communism" is not a movement of the downtrodden masses but is a movement created, manipulated and used by power-seeking billionaires in order to gain control over the world . . . first by establishing socialist governments in the various nations and then consolidating them all through a "Great Merger," into an all-powerful world socialist super-state probably under the auspices of the United Nations. The balance of this book will outline just how they have used Communism to approach that goal.

Chapter III

The Money Manipulators

M*ANY* college history professors tell their charges that the books they will be using in the class are "objective." But stop and ask yourself: Is it possible to write a history book without a particular point of view? There are billions of events which take place in the world each day. To think of writing a complete history of a nation covering even a year is absolutely incredible.

Not only is a historian's ability to write an "objective" history limited by the sheer volume of happenings but by the fact that many of the most important happenings never appear in the papers or even in somebody's memoirs. The decisions reached by the "Big Boys" in the smoke-filled rooms are not reported even in the *New York Times* which ostensibly reports all the news that is fit to print. ("All the news that fits" is a more accurate description.)

In order to build his case, a historian must select a miniscule number of facts from the limited number that are known. If he does not have a "theory," how does he separate important facts from unimportant ones? As Professor Stuart Crane has pointed out, this is why every book "proves" the author's thesis. But no book is objective. No book can be objective;

and this book is not objective. (Liberal reviewers should have a ball quoting that out of context.) The information in it is true, but the book is not objective. We have carefully selected the facts to prove our case. We believe that most other historians have focused on the landscape, and ignored that which is most important: the cart, boy and donkey.

Most of the facts which we bring out are readily verifiable at any large library. But our contention is that we have arranged these facts in the order which most accurately reveals their true significance in history. These are the facts the Establishment does not want you to know.

Have you ever had the experience of walking into a mystery movie two-thirds of the way through? Confusing wasn't it? All the evidence made it look as if the butler were the murderer, but in the final scenes you find out, surprisingly, that it was the man's wife all along. You have to stay and see the beginning of the film. Then as all the pieces fall into place, the story makes sense.

This situation is very similar to the one in which millions of Americans find themselves today. They are confused by current happenings in the nation. They have come in as the movie, so to speak, is going into its conclusion. The earlier portion of the mystery is needed to make the whole thing understandable. (Actually, we are not really starting at the beginning, but we are going back far enough to give meaning to today's happenings.)

In order to understand the conspiracy it is necessary to have some rudimentary knowledge of banking and, particularly, of international bankers. While it would be on over-simplification to ascribe the entire conspiracy to international bankers, they nevertheless have played a key role. Think of the conspiracy as a hand with one finger labelled "international banking," others "foundations," "the anti-religion movement" "Fabian Socialism," and "Communism." But it was the international bankers of whom Professor Quigley was speaking when we quoted him earlier as stating that their aim was

44

nothing less than control of the world through finance.

Where do governments get the enormous amounts of money they need? Most, of course, comes from taxation; but governments often spend more than they are willing to tax from their citizens and so are forced to borrow. Our national debt is now $455 billion—every cent of it borrowed at interest from somewhere.

The public is led to believe that our government borrows from "the people" through savings bonds. Actually, only the smallest percentage of the national debt is held by individuals in this form. Most government bonds, except those owned by the government itself through its trust funds, are held by vast banking firms known as international banks.[1]

For centuries there has been big money to be made by international bankers in the financing of governments and kings. Such operators are faced, however, with certain thorny problems. We know that smaller banking operations protect themselves by taking collateral, but what kind of collateral can you get from a government or a king? What if the banker comes to collect and the king says, "Off with his head"? The process through which one collects a debt from a government or a monarch is not a subject taught in the business schools of our universities, and most of us—never having been in the business of financing kings—have not given the problem much thought. But there is a king-financing business and to those who can ensure collection it is lucrative indeed.

Economics Professor Stuart Crane notes that there are two means used to collateralize loans to governments and kings. Whenever a business firm borrows big money its creditor obtains a voice in management to protect his investment. Like a business, no government can borrow big money unless willing to surrender to the creditor some measure of sovereignty as collateral. Certainly international bankers who have loaned hundreds of billions of dollars to governments around the world command considerable influence in the policies of such governments.

But the ultimate advantage the creditor has over the king or president is that if the ruler gets out of line the banker can finance his enemy or rival. Therefore, if you want to stay in the lucrative king-financing business, it is wise to have an enemy or rival waiting in the wings to unseat every king or president to whom you lend. If the king doesn't have an enemy, you must create one.

Preeminent in playing this game was the famous House of Rothschild. Its founder, Meyer Amschel Rothschild (1743-1812) of Frankfurt, Germany, kept one of his five sons at home to run the Frankfurt bank and sent the others to London, Paris, Vienna and Naples. The Rothschilds became incredibly wealthy during the nineteenth century by financing governments to fight each other. According to Professor Stuart Crane:

> "If you will look back at every war in Europe during the Nineteenth Century, you will see that they always ended with the establishment of a 'balance of power.' With every re-shuffling there was a balance of power in a new grouping around the House of Rothschild in England, France, or Austria. They grouped nations so that if any king got out of line a war would break out and the war would be decided by which way the financing went. Researching the debt positions of the warring nations will usually indicate who was to be punished."

In describing the characteristics of the Rothschilds and other major international bankers, Dr. Quigley tells us that they remained different from ordinary bankers in several ways: they were cosmopolitan and international; they were close to governments and were particularly concerned with government debts, including foreign government debts; these bankers came to be called "international bankers." (Quigley, p. 52)

One major reason for the historical blackout on the role of the international bankers in political history is that the

Rothschilds were Jewish. Anti-Semites have played into the hands of the conspiracy by trying to portray the entire conspiracy as Jewish. Nothing could be farther from the truth. The traditionally Anglo-Saxon J. P. Morgan and Rockefeller international banking institutions have played a key role in the conspiracy. But there is no denying the importance of the Rothschilds and their satellites. However, it is just as unreasonable and immoral to blame all Jews for the crimes of the Rothschilds as it is to hold all Baptists accountable for the crimes of the Rockefellers.

The Jewish members of the conspiracy have used an organization called the Anti-Defamation League as an instrument to try to convince everyone that any mention of the Rothschilds or their allies is an attack on all Jews. In this way they have stifled almost all honest scholarship on international bankers and made the subject taboo within universities.

Any individual or book exploring this subject is immediately attacked by hundreds of A.D.L. communities all over the country. The A.D.L. has never let truth or logic interfere with its highly professional smear jobs. When no evidence is apparent, the A.D.L., which staunchly opposed so-called "McCarthyism," accuses people of being "latent anti-Semites." Can you imagine how they would yowl and scream if someone accused them of being "latent" Communists?

Actually, nobody has a right to be more angry at the Rothschild clique than their fellow Jews. The Warburgs, part of the Rothschild empire, helped finance Adolph Hitler. There were few if any Rothschilds or Warburgs in the Nazi prison camps! They sat out the war in luxurious hotels in Paris or emigrated to the United States or England. As a group, Jews have suffered most at the hands of these power seekers. A Rothschild has much more in common with a Rockefeller than he does with a tailor from Budapest or the Bronx.

Since the keystone of the international banking empires has been government bonds, it has been in the interest of these international bankers to encourage government debt. The higher the debt the more the interest. Nothing drives government deeply into debt like a war; and it has not been an uncommon practice among international bankers to finance both sides of the bloodiest military conflicts. For example, during our Civil War the North was financed by the Rothschilds through their American agent, August Belmont, and the American South through the Erlangers, Rothschild relatives.[2]

But while wars and revolutions have been useful to international bankers in gaining or increasing control over governments, the key to such control has always been control of money. You can control a government if you have it in your debt; a creditor is in a position to demand the privileges of monopoly from the sovereign. Money-seeking governments have granted monopolies in state banking, natural resources, oil concessions and transportation. However, the monopoly which the international financiers most covet is control over a nation's money.

Eventually these international bankers actually owned as private corporations the central banks of the various European nations. The Bank of England, Bank of France and Bank of Germany were not owned by their respective governments, as almost everyone imagines, but were privately owned monopolies granted by the heads of state, usually in return for loans. Under this system, observed Reginald McKenna, President of the Midlands Bank of England: "Those that create and issue the money and credit direct the policies of government and hold in their hands the destiny of the people."[3] Once the government is in debt to the bankers it is at their mercy. A frightening example was cited by the *London Financial Times* of September 26, 1921, which revealed that even at that time: "Half a dozen men at the top of the Big Five Banks could upset the whole fabric of government finance by refraining from renewing Treasury Bills."

All those who have sought dictatorial control over modern nations have understood the necessity of a central bank. When the League of Just Men hired a hack revolutionary named Karl Marx to write a blueprint for conquest called *The Communist Manifesto*, the fifth plank read: "Centralization of credit in the hands of the state, by means of a national bank with state capital and an exclusive monopoly."④ Lenin later said that the establishment of a central bank was ninety percent of communizing a country. Such conspirators knew that you cannot take control of a nation without military force unless that nation has a central bank through which you can control its economy. The anarchist Bakunin sarcastically remarked about the followers of Karl Marx: "They have one foot in the bank and one foot in the socialist movement."⑤

The international financiers set up their own front man in charge of each of Europe's central banks. Professor Quigley reports:

> "It must not be felt that these heads of the world's chief central banks were themselves substantive powers in world finance. They were not. Rather, they were the technicians and agents of the dominant investment bankers of their own countries, who had raised them up and were perfectly capable of throwing them down. The substantive financial powers of the world were in the hands of these investment bankers (also called 'international' or 'merchants' bankers) who remained largely behind the scenes in their own unincorporated private banks. These formed a system of international cooperation and national dominance which was more private, more powerful, and more secret than that of their agents in the central banks. . . ." (p. 326-7)

Dr. Quigley also reveals that the international bankers who owned and controlled the Banks of England and France maintained their power even after those Banks were theoretically socialized.

Naturally those who controlled the central banks of Europe were eager from the start to fasten a similar establishment on the United States. From the earliest days, the Founding Fathers had been conscious of attempts to control America through money manipulation, and they carried on a running battle with the international bankers. Thomas Jefferson wrote to John Adams: ". . . I sincerely believe, with you, that banking establishments are more dangerous than standing armies. . . ."[6]

But, even though America did not have a central bank after President Jackson abolished it in 1836, the European financiers and their American agents managed to obtain a great deal of control over our monetary system. Gustavus Myers, in his *History of the Great American Fortunes*, reveals:

> "Under the surface, the Rothschilds long had a powerful influence in dictating American financial laws. The law records show that they were powers in the old Bank of the United States [abolished by Andrew Jackson]."[7]

During the nineteenth century the leading financiers of the metropolitan East often cut one another's financial throats, but as their Western and rural victims started to organize politically, the "robber barons" saw that they had a "community of interest" toward which they must work together to protect themselves from thousands of irate farmers and up and coming competitors. This diffusion of economic power was one of the main factors stimulating the demands for a central bank by would-be business and financial monopolists.

In *Years of Plunder* Proctor Hansl writes of this era:

> "Among the Morgans, Kuhn-Loebs and other similar pillars of the industrial order there was less disposition to become involved in disagreements that led to financial dislocation. A community of interest came into being, with results that were highly

beneficial. . . .[8]

But aside from the major Eastern centers, most American bankers and their customers still distrusted the whole concept.

In order to show the hinterlands that they were going to need a central banking system, the international bankers created a series of panics as a demonstration of their power—a warning of what would happen unless the rest of the bankers got into line. The man in charge of conducting these lessons was J. Pierpont Morgan, American-born but educated in England and Germany. Morgan is referred to by many, including Congressman Louis McFadden (a banker who for ten years headed the House Banking and Currency Committee), as the top American agent of the English Rothschilds.

By the turn of the century J. P. Morgan was already an old hand at creating artificial panics. Such affairs were well coordinated. Senator Robert Owen, a co-author of the Federal Reserve Act (who later deeply regretted his role), testified before a Congressional Committee that the bank he owned received from the National Bankers' Association what came to be known as the "Panic Circular of 1893." It stated: "You will at once retire one-third of your circulation and call in one-half of your loans. . . ."[9]

Historian Frederick Lewis Allen tells in *Life* magazine of April 25, 1949, of Morgan's role in spreading rumors about the insolvency of the Knickerbocker Bank and The Trust Company of America, which rumors triggered the 1907 panic. In answer to the question: "Did Morgan precipitate the panic?" Allen reports:

> "Oakleigh Thorne, the president of that particular trust company, testified later before a congressional committee that his bank had been subjected to only moderate withdrawals . . . that he had not applied for help, and that it was the [Morgan's] 'sore point' statement alone that had caused the run on his bank.

51

From this testimony, plus the disciplinary measures taken by the Clearing House against the Heinze, Morse and Thomas banks, plus other fragments of supposedly pertinent evidence, certain chroniclers have arrived at the ingenious conclusion that the Morgan interests took advantage of the unsettled conditions during the autumn of 1907 to precipitate the panic, guiding it shrewdly as it progressed so that it would kill off rival banks and consolidate the preeminence of the banks within the Morgan orbit."

The "panic" which Morgan had created, he proceeded to end almost single-handedly. He had made his point. Frederick Allen explains:

> "The lesson of the Panic of 1907 was clear, though not for some six years was it destined to be embodied in legislation: the United States gravely needed a central banking system. . . ."

The man who was to play the most significant part in providing America with that central bank was Paul Warburg, who along with his brother Felix had immigrated to the United States from Germany in 1902. (See Chart 4.) They left brother Max (later a major financier of the Russian Revolution) at home in Frankfurt to run the family bank (M. N. Warburg & Company).

Paul Warburg married Nina Loeb, daughter of Solomon Loeb of Kuhn, Loeb and Company, America's most powerful international banking firm. Brother Felix married Frieda Schiff, daughter of Jacob Schiff, the ruling power behind Kuhn, Loeb. Stephen Birmingham writes in his authoritative *Our Crowd*: "In the eighteenth century the Schiffs and Rothschilds shared a double house" in Frankfurt. Schiff reportedly bought his partnership in Kuhn, Loeb with Rothschild money.

Both Paul and Felix Warburg became partners in Kuhn,

Loeb and Company.

In 1907, the year of the Morgan-precipitated panic, Paul Warburg began spending almost all of his time writing and lecturing on the need for "bank reform." Kuhn, Loeb and Company was sufficiently public spirited about the matter to keep him on salary at $500,000 per year while for the next six years he donated his time to "the public good."

Working with Warburg in promoting this "banking reform" was Nelson Aldrich, known as "Morgan's floor broker in the Senate." Aldrich's daughter Abby married John D. Rockefeller Jr. (the current Governor of New York is named for his maternal grandfather).

After the Panic of 1907, Aldrich was appointed by the Senate to head the National Monetary Commission. Although he had no technical knowledge of banking, Aldrich and his entourage spent nearly two years and $300,000 of the taxpayers' money being wined and dined by the owners of Europe's central banks as they toured the Continent "studying" central banking. When the Commission returned from its luxurious junket it held no meetings and made no report for nearly two years. But Senator Aldrich was busy "arranging" things. Together with Paul Warburg and other international bankers, he staged one of the most important secret meetings in the history of the United States. Rockefeller agent Frank Vanderlip admitted many years later in his memoirs:

> "Despite my views about the value to society of greater publicity for the affairs of corporations, there was an occasion, near the close of 1910, when I was as secretive—indeed as furtive—as any conspirator. . . . I do not feel it is any exaggeration to speak of our secret expedition to Jekyl Island as the occasion of the actual conception of what eventually became the Federal Reserve System."[10]

The secrecy was well warranted. At stake was control over

53

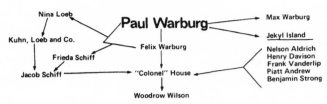

FEDERAL RESERVE

Nina Loeb

Kuhn, Loeb and Co.

Frieda Schiff

Jacob Schiff

Paul Warburg

Felix Warburg

"Colonel" House

Woodrow Wilson

Max Warburg

Jekyl Island

Nelson Aldrich
Henry Davison
Frank Vanderlip
Piatt Andrew
Benjamin Strong

the entire economy. Senator Aldrich had issued confidential invitations to Henry P. Davison of J. P. Morgan & Company; Frank A. Vanderlip, President of the Rockefeller-owned National City Bank; A. Piatt Andrew, Assistant Secretary of the Treasury; Benjamin Strong of Morgan's Bankers Trust Company; and Paul Warburg. They were all to accompany him to Jekyl Island, Georgia, to write the final recommendations of the National Monetary Commission report.

At Jekyl Island, writes B. C. Forbes in his *Men Who Are Making America*:

> "After a general discussion it was decided to draw up certain broad principles on which all could agree. Every member of the group voted for a central bank as being the ideal cornerstone for any banking system."

Warburg stressed that the name "central bank" must be

avoided at all costs. It was decided to promote the scheme as a "regional reserve" system with four (later twelve) branches in different sections of the country. The conspirators knew that the New York bank would dominate the rest, which would be marble "white elephants" to deceive the public.

Out of the Jekyl Island meeting came the completion of the Monetary Commission Report and the Aldrich Bill. Warburg had proposed the bill be designated the "Federal Reserve System," but Aldrich insisted his own name was already associated in the public's mind with banking reform and that it would arouse suspicion if a bill were introduced which did not bear his name. However, Aldrich's name attached to the bill proved to be the kiss of death, since any law bearing his name was so obviously a project of the international bankers.

When the Aldrich Bill could not be pushed through Congress, a new strategy had to be devised. The Republican Party was too closely connected with Wall Street. The only hope for a central bank was to disguise it and have it put through by the Democrats as a measure to strip Wall Street of its power. The opportunity to do this came with the approach of the 1912 Presidental election. Republican President William Howard Taft, who had turned against the Aldrich Bill, seemed a sure-fire bet for re-election until Taft's predecessor, fellow Republican Teddy Roosevelt, agreed to run on the ticket of the Progressive Party. In *America's 60 Families*, Ferdinand Lundberg acknowledges:

> "As soon as Roosevelt signified that he would again challenge Taft the President's defeat was inevitable. Throughout the three-cornered fight [Taft-Roosevelt-Wilson] Roosevelt had [Morgan agents Frank] Munsey and [George] Perkins constantly at his heels, supplying money, going over his speeches, bringing people from Wall Street in to help, and, in general, carrying the entire burden of the campaign against Taft. . . .

Perkins and J. P. Morgan and Company were the substance of the Progressive Party; everything else was trimming. . . .

In short, most of Roosevelt's campaign fund was supplied by the two Morgan hatchet men who were seeking Taft's scalp."

The Democratic candidate, Woodrow Wilson, was equally the property of Morgan. Dr. Gabriel Kolko in his *The Triumph of Conservatism*, reports: "In late 1907 he [Wilson] supported the Aldrich Bill on banking, and was full of praise for Morgan's role in American society." According to Lundberg: "For nearly twenty years before his nomination Woodrow Wilson had moved in the shadow of Wall Street."

Woodrow Wilson and Teddy Roosevelt proceeded to whistle-stop the country trying to out-do each other in florid (and hypocritical) denunciations of the Wall Street "money trust"—the same group of *Insiders* which was financing the campaigns of both.

Dr. Kolko goes on to tell us that, at the beginning of 1912, banking reform "seemed a dead issue. . . . The banking reform movement had neatly isolated itself." Wilson resurrected the issue and promised the country a money system free from domination by the international bankers of Wall Street. Moreover, the Democrat platform expressly stated: "We are opposed to the Aldrich plan for a central bank." But the "Big Boys" knew who they had bought. Among the international financiers who contributed heavily to the Wilson campaign, in addition to those already named, were Jacob Schiff, Bernard Baruch, Henry Morgenthau, Thomas Fortune Ryan, and *New York Times* publisher Adolph Ochs.

The *Insiders'* sheepdog who controlled Wilson and guided the program through Congress was the mysterious "Colonel" Edward Mandel House, the British-educated son of a representative of England's financial interests in the American South. The title was honorary; House never served in the military. He was strictly a behind-the-scenes wire-puller and is regarded by many historians as the real President of the United States during the Wilson years. House authored a book, *Philip Dru: Administrator*, in which he wrote of establishing "Socialism as dreamed by Karl Marx." As steps toward his goal, House, both in his book and in real life, called for passage of a graduated income tax and a central bank providing "a flexible [inflatable paper] currency." The graduated income tax and a central bank are two of the ten planks of *The Communist Manifesto*.

In his *The Intimate Papers of Colonel House*, Professor Charles Seymour refers to the "Colonel" as the "unseen guardian angel" of the Federal Reserve Act. Seymour's work contains numerous documents and records showing constant contact between House and Paul Warburg while the Federal Reserve Act was being prepared and steered through Congress. Biographer George Viereck assures us that "The Schiffs, the Warburgs, the Kahns, the Rockefellers, and the Morgans put their faith in House. . . ."[11] Their faith was amply rewarded.

In order to support the fiction that the Federal Reserve Act was a "people's bill," the *Insider* financiers put up a smoke-screen of opposition to it. It was strictly a case of Br'er Rabbit begging not to be thrown into the briar patch. Both Aldrich and Vanderlip denounced what in actuality was their own bill. Nearly twenty-five years later Frank Vanderlip admitted: "Now although the Aldrich Federal Reserve Plan was defeated when it bore the name Aldrich, nevertheless its essential points were all contained in the plan that finally was adopted."[12]

Taking advantage of Congress' desire to adjourn for Christmas, the Federal Reserve Act was passed on December 22, 1913 by a vote of 298 to 60 in the House, and in the Senate by a majority of 43 to 25. Wilson had fulfilled to the *Insiders* the pledge he had made in order to become President. Warburg told House, "Well, it hasn't got quite everything we want, but the lack can be adjusted later by administrative process."

There was genuine opposition to the Act, but it could not match the power of the bill's advocates. Conservative Henry Cabot Lodge Sr. proclaimed with great foresight, "The bill as it stands seems to me to open the way to a vast inflation of currency. . . . I do not like to think that any law can be passed which will make it possible to submerge the gold standard in a flood of irredeemable paper currency." (*Congressional Record*, June 10, 1932.) After the vote, Congressman Charles A. Lindbergh Sr., father of the famous aviator, told Congress:

> "This act establishes the most gigantic trust on earth. . . . When the President signs this act the invisible government by the money power, proven to exist by the Money Trust investigation, will be legalized. . . .
> This is the Aldrich Bill in disguise. . . .
> The new law will create inflation whenever the trusts want inflation. . . ."[13]

The Federal Reserve Act was, and still is, hailed as a victory of "democracy" over the "money trust." Nothing could be farther from the truth.

The whole central bank concept was engineered by the very group it was supposed to strip of power. The myth that the "money trust" had been defrocked should have been exploded when Paul Warburg was appointed to the first Federal Reserve Board—a board which was handpicked by "Colonel" House. Paul Warburg relinquished his $500,000 a year job as a Kuhn, Loeb partner to take a $12,000 a year job with the Federal Reserve. The "accidentalists" who teach in our universities would have you believe that he did it because he was a "public spirited citizen." And the man who served as Chairman of the New York Federal Reserve Bank during its early critical years was the same Benjamin Strong of the Morgan interests, who accompanied Warburg, Davison, Vanderlip *et al.* to Jekyl Island, Georgia, to draft the Aldrich Bill.

How powerful is our "central bank?" The Federal Reserve controls our money supply and interest rates, and thereby manipulates the entire economy—creating inflation or deflation, recession or boom, and sending the stock market up or down at whim. The Federal Reserve is so powerful that Congressman Wright Patman, Chairman of the House Banking Committee, maintains:

> "In the United States today we have in effect two governments. . . . We have the duly constituted Government. . . . Then we have an independent, uncontrolled and uncoordinated government in the Federal Reserve System, operating the money powers which are reserved to Congress by the Constitution."[14]

Neither Presidents, Congressmen nor Secretaries of the Treasury direct the Federal Reserve! In the matters of money, the Federal Reserve directs them! The uncontrolled power of the "Fed" was admitted by Secretary of the Treasury David M. Kennedy in an interview for the May 5, 1969, issue of *U. S. News & World Report:*

> "Q. Do you approve of the latest credit-tightening moves?
>
> A. It's not my job to approve or disapprove. It is the action of the Federal Reserve."

And, curiously enough, the Federal Reserve System has never been audited and has firmly resisted all attempts by House Banking Committee Chairman Wright Patman to have it audited. (*N. Y. Times*, Sept. 14, 1967.)

How successful has the Federal Reserve System been? It depends on your point of view. Since Woodrow Wilson took his oath of office, the national debt has risen from $1 billion

Prof. Carroll Quigley of Harvard, Princeton and Georgetown Universities wrote book disclosing international bankers' plan to control the world from behind the political and financial scenes. Quigley revealed plans of billionaires to establish dictatorship of the super-rich disguised as workers' democracies.

J. P. Morgan created artificial panic used as excuse to pass Federal Reserve Act. Morgan was instrumental in pushing U. S. into WWI to protect his loans to British government. He financed Socialist groups to create an all-powerful centralized government which international bankers would control at the apex from behind the scenes. After his death, his partners helped finance the Bolshevik Revolution in Russia.

to $455 billion. The total amount of interest paid since then to the international bankers holding that debt is staggering, with interest having become the third largest item in the federal budget. Interest on the national debt is now $22 billion every year, and climbing steeply as inflation pushes up the interest rate on government bonds. Meanwhile, our gold is mortgaged to European central banks, and our silver has all been sold. With economic catastrophe imminent, only a blind disciple of the "accidental theory of history" could believe that all of this occurred by coincidence.

When the Federal Reserve System was foisted on an unsuspecting American public, there were absolute guarantees that there would be no more boom and bust economic cycles. The men who, behind the scenes, were pushing the central bank concept for the international bankers faithfully promised that from then on there would be only steady growth and perpetual prosperity. However, Congressman Charles A. Lindberg Sr. accurately proclaimed: "From now on depressions will be scientifically created."[15]

Using a central bank to create alternate periods of inflation and deflation, and thus whipsawing the public for vast profit, had been worked out by the international bankers to an exact science.

Having built the Federal Reserve as a tool to consolidate and control wealth, the international bankers were now ready for a major killing. Between 1923 and 1929, the Federal Reserve expanded (inflated) the money supply by sixty-two percent. Much of this new money was used to bid the stock market up to dizzying heights.[16]

At the same time that enormous amounts of credit money were being made available, the mass media began to ballyhoo tales of the instant riches to be made in the stock market. According to Ferdinand Lundberg:

> "For profits to be made on these funds the public had to be induced to speculate, and it was so in-

duced by misleading newspaper accounts, many of
them bought and paid for by the brokers that oper-
ated the pools. . . ."[17]

The House Hearings on Stabilization of the Purchasing
Power of the Dollar disclosed evidence in 1928 that the Federal Reserve Board was working closely with the heads of
European central banks. The Committee warned that a major
crash had been planned in 1927. At a secret luncheon of the
Federal Reserve Board and heads of the European central
banks, the committee warned, the international bankers were
tightening the noose.

Montagu Norman, Governor of the Bank of England, came
to Washington on February 6, 1929, to confer with Andrew
Mellon, Secretary of the Treasury. On November 11, 1927,
the *Wall Street Journal* described Mr. Norman as "the currency dictator of Europe." Professor Carroll Quigley notes
that Norman, a close confidant of J. P. Morgan, admitted: "I
hold the hegemony of the world." Immediately after this
mysterious visit, the Federal Reserve Board reversed its easy-
money policy and began raising the discount rate. The balloon
which had been inflated constantly for nearly seven years was
about to be exploded.

On October 24, the feathers hit the fan. Writing in *The
United States' Unresolved Monetary and Political Problems*,
William Bryan describes what happened:

"When everything was ready, the New York financiers started calling 24 hour broker call loans.
This meant that the stock brokers and the customers
had to dump their stock on the market in order to
pay the loans. This naturally collapsed the stock
market and brought a banking collapse all over the
country because the banks not owned by the oligarchy were heavily involved in broker call claims at
this time, and bank runs soon exhausted their coin

and currency and they had to close. The Federal Reserve System would not come to their aid, although they were instructed under the law to maintain an elastic currency."[18]

The investing public, including most stock brokers and bankers, took a horrendous blow in the crash, but not the *Insiders*. They were either out of the market or had sold "short" so that they made enormous profits as the Dow Jones plummeted. For those who knew the score, a comment by Paul Warburg had provided the warning to sell. That signal came on March 9, 1929, when the *Financial Chronical* quoted Warburg as giving this sound advice:

> "If orgies of unrestricted speculation are permitted to spread too far . . . the ultimate collapse is certain . . . to bring about a general depression involving the whole country."

Sharpies were later able to buy back these stocks at a ninety percent discount from their former highs.

To think that the scientifically engineered Crash of '29 was an accident or the result of stupidity defies all logic. The international bankers who promoted the inflationary policies and pushed the propaganda which pumped up the stock market represented too many generations of accumulated expertise to have blundered into "the great depression."

Congressman Louis McFadden, Chairman of the House Banking and Currency Committee, commented:

> "It [the depression] was not accidental. It was a carefully contrived occurrence. . . . The international bankers sought to bring about a condition of despair here so that they might emerge as the rulers of us all."[19]

Although we have not had another depression of the magnitude of that which followed 1929, we have since suffered regular recessions. Each of these has followed a period in which the Federal Reserve tromped down hard on the money accelerator and then slammed on the brakes. Since 1929 the following recessions have been created by such manipulation:

1936-1937 —Stock prices fell fifty percent;
1948   —Stock prices dropped sixteen percent;
1953   —Stock declined thirteen percent;
1956-1957 —The market dipped thirteen percent;
1957   —Late in the year the market plunged nineteen percent;
1960   —The market was off seventeen percent;
1966   —Stock prices plummeted twenty-five percent;
1970   —The market plunged over twenty-five percent.

Chart 5, based on one appearing in the highly respected financial publication, *Indicator Digest* of June 24, 1969, shows the effects on the Dow-Jones Industrial Average of Federal Reserve policies of expanding or restricting the monetary supply. This is how the stock market is manipulated and how depressions or recessions are scientifically created. If you have inside knowledge as to which way the Federal Reserve policy is going to go, you can make a ton of money.

The members of the Federal Reserve Board are appointed by the President for fourteen year terms. Since these positions control the entire economy of the country they are far more important than cabinet positions, but who has ever heard of any of them except possibly Chairman Arthur Burns? These appointments which should be extensively debated by the Senate are routinely approved. But, here, as in Europe, these men are mere figureheads, put in their positions at the behest of the international bankers who finance the Presidential cam-

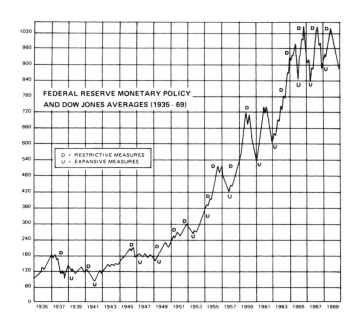

FEDERAL RESERVE MONETARY POLICY
AND DOW JONES AVERAGES (1935 - 69)

D = RESTRICTIVE MEASURES
U = EXPANSIVE MEASURES

paigns of both political parties.

And, Professor Quigley reveals that these international bankers who owned and controlled the Banks of England and France maintained their power even after those banks were theoretically socialized. The American system is slightly different, but the net effect is the same—ever-increasing debt requiring ever-increasing interest payments, inflation and periodic scientifically created depressions and recessions.

The end result, if the *Insiders* have their way, will be the dream of Montagu Norman of the Bank of England "that the Hegemony of World Finance should reign supreme over everyone, everywhere, as one whole super-national control mechanism."[20]

Chapter IV

Bankrolling the Bolshevik Revolution

*T*HE *ESTABLISHING* of the Federal Reserve System provided the "conspiracy" with an instrument whereby the international bankers could run the national debt up to the sky,
thereby collecting enormous amounts of interest and also gaining control over the borrower. During the Wilson Administration alone, the national debt expanded 800 percent.

Two months prior to the passage of the Federal Reserve
Act, the conspirators had created the mechanism to collect the
funds to pay the interest on the national debt. That mecha-
nism was the progressive income tax, the second plank of Karl
Marx' *Communist Manifesto* which contained ten planks for
SOCIALIZING a country.

One quite naturally assumes that the graduated income tax
would be opposed by the wealthy. The fact is that many of
the wealthiest Americans supported it. Some, no doubt, out of
altruism and because, at first, the taxes were very small. But
others backed the scheme because they already had a plan for
permanently avoiding both the income tax and the subsequent
inheritance tax.

What happened was this: At the turn of the century the
Populists, a group of rural socialists, were gaining strength and

challenging the power of the New York bankers and monopolist industrialists. While the Populists had the wrong answers, they asked many of the right questions. Unfortunately, they were led to believe that the banker-monopolist control over government, which they opposed, was a product of free enterprise.

Since the Populist threat to the cartelists was from the Left (there being no organized political movement for *laissez-faire*), the *Insiders* moved to capture the Left. Professor Quigley discloses that over fifty years ago the Morgan firm decided to infiltrate the Leftwing political movement in the United States. This was not difficult to do since these Left groups needed funds and were eager for help to get their message to the public. Wall Street supplied both. There was nothing new about this decision, says Quigley, since other financiers had talked about it and even attempted it earlier. He continues:

> "What made it decisively important this time was the combination of its adoption by the dominant Wall Street financier, at a time when tax policy was driving all financiers to seek tax-exempt refuges for their fortunes. . . ." (Page 938)

Radical movements are never successful unless they attract big money and/or outside support. The great historian of the Twentieth Century, Oswald Spengler, was one of those who saw what American Liberals refused to see—that the Left is controlled by its alleged enemy, the malefactors of great wealth. He wrote in his monumental *Decline of the West* (Modern Library, New York, 1945):

> "There is no proletarian, not even a Communist, movement, that has not operated in the interests of money, in the direction indicated by money, and for the time being permitted by money—and that without the idealists among its leaders having the slight-

est suspicion of the fact."

While the Populist movement was basically non-conspiratorial, its Leftist ideology and platform were made to order for the elitist *Insiders* because it aimed at concentrating power in government. The *Insiders* knew they could control that power and use it to their own purposes. They were not, of course, interested in promoting competition but in restricting it. Professor Gabriel Kolko has prepared a lengthy volume presenting the undeniable proof that the giant corporate manipulators *promoted* much of the so-called "progressive legislation" of the Roosevelt and Wilson eras—legislation which ostensibly was aimed at controlling their abuses, but which was so written as to suit their interests. In *The Triumph of Conservatism* (by which Kolko mistakenly means big business), he notes:

> ". . . the significant reason for many businessmen welcoming and working to increase federal intervention into their affairs has been virtually ignored by historians and economists. The oversight was due to the illusion that American industry was centralized and monopolized to such an extent that it could rationalize the activity [regulate production and prices] in its various branches voluntarily. Quite the opposite was true. Despite the large numbers of mergers, and the growth in the absolute size of many corporations, the dominant tendency in the American economy at the beginning of this century was toward growing competition. Competition was unacceptable to many key business and financial interests. . . ."①

The best way for the *Insiders* to eliminate this growing competition was to impose a progressive income tax on their competitors while writing the laws so as to include built-in escape hatches for themselves. Actually, very few of the proponents of the graduated income tax realized they were playing into the hands of those they were seeking to control. As Ferdinand Lundberg notes in *The Rich And The Super-Rich:*

> "What it [the income tax] became, finally, was a siphon gradually inserted into the pocketbooks of the general public. Imposed to popular huzzas as a class tax, the income tax was gradually turned into a mass tax in a jiujitsu turnaround. . . ."②

The *Insiders'* principal mouthpiece in the Senate during this period was Nelson Aldrich, one of the conspirators involved in engineering the creation of the Federal Reserve and the maternal grandfather of Nelson Aldrich Rockefeller. Lundberg says that "When Aldrich spoke, newsmen understood that although the words were his, the dramatic line was surely approved by 'Big John [D. Rockefeller]. . . .' " In earlier years Aldrich had denounced the income tax as "communistic and socialistic," but in 1909 he pulled a dramatic and stunning reversal. The *American Biographical Dictionary* comments:

> "Just when the opposition had become formidable he [Aldrich] took the wind out of its sails by bringing forward, with the support of the President [Taft], a proposed amendment to the Constitution empowering Congress to lay income taxes."

Howard Hinton records in his biography of Cordell Hull that Congressman Hull, who had been pushing in the House for the income tax, wrote this stunned observation:

> "During the past few weeks the unexpected spectacle of certain so-called 'old-line conservative' [sic] Republican leaders in Congress suddenly reversing their attitude of a lifetime and seemingly espousing, through ill-concealed reluctance, the proposed in-

70

come-tax amendment to the Constitution has been the occasion of universal surprise and wonder."③

The escape hatch for the *Insiders* to avoid paying taxes was ready. By the time the Amendment had been approved by the states (even before the income-tax was passed), the Rockefellers and Carnegie foundations were in full operation.

One must remember that it was to break up the Standard Oil (Rockefeller) and U. S. Steel (Carnegie) monopolies that the various ant-trust acts were ostensibly passed. These monopolists could now compound their wealth tax-free while competitors had to face a graduated income tax which made it difficult to amass capital. As we have said, socialism is not a share-the-wealth program, as the socialists would like you to believe, but a consolidate-and-control-the-wealth program for the *Insiders*. The Reece Committee which investigated foundations for Congress in 1953 proved with an overwhelming amount of evidence that the various Rockefeller and Carnegie foundations have been promoting socialism since their inception. (See Rene Wormser's *Foundations: Their Power and Influence*, Devin Adair, New York, 1958.)

The conspirators now had created the mechanisms to run up the debt, to collect the debt, and (for themselves) to avoid the taxes required to pay the yearly interest on the debt. Then all that was needed was a reason to escalate the debt. Nothing runs up a national debt like a war. And World War I was being brewed in Europe.

In 1916, Woodrow Wilson was re-elected by a hair. He had based his campaign on the slogan: "He Kept Us Out of War!" The American public was extremely opposed to America's getting involved in a European war. Staying out of the perennial foreign quarrels had been an American tradition since George Washington. But as Wilson was stumping the country giving his solemn word that American soldiers would not be sent into a foreign war, he was preparing to do just the opposite. His "alter ego," as he called "Colonel" House, was making behind-the-scenes agreements with England which committed America to entering the war. Just five months later we were in it. The same crowd which manipulated the passage of the income tax and the Federal Reserve System wanted America in the war. J. P. Morgan, John D. Rockefeller, "Colonel" House, Jacob Schiff, Paul Warburg and the rest of the Jekyl Island conspirators were all deeply involved in getting us involved. Many of these financiers had loaned England large sums of money. In fact, J. P. Morgan & Co. served as British financial agents in this country during World War I.

While all of the standard reasons given for the outbreak of World War I in Europe doubtless were factors, there were also other more important causes. The conspiracy had been planning the war for over two decades. The assassination of an Austrian Archduke was merely an incident providing an excuse for starting a chain reaction.

After years of fighting, the war was a complete stalemate and would have ended almost immediately in a negotiated settlement (as had most other European conflicts) had not the U. S. declared war on Germany.

As soon as Wilson's re-election had been engineered through the "he kept us out of war" slogan, a complete reversal of propaganda was instituted. In those days before radio and television, public opinion was controlled almost exclusively by newspapers. Many of the major newspapers were controlled by the Federal Reserve crowd. Now they began beating the drums over the "inevitability of war." Arthur Ponsonby, a member of the British Parliament, admitted in his book *Falsehood In War Time* (E. P. Dutton & Co., Inc., New York, 1928): "There must have been more deliberate lying in the world from 1914 to 1918 than in any other period of the world's history."[4] Propaganda concerning the war was heavily one-sided. Although after the war many historians admitted that one side was as guilty as the other in starting the war, Germany was pictured as a militaristic monster which wanted to rule the world. Remember, this picture was painted by Britain which had its soldiers in more countries around the world than all other nations put together. So-called "Prussian militarism" did exist, but it was no threat to conquer the world. Meanwhile, the sun never set on the British Empire! Actually, the Germans were proving to be tough business competitors in the world's markets and the British did not approve.

In order to generate war fever, the sinking of the Lusitania —a British ship torpedoed two years earlier—was revived and given renewed headlines. German submarine warfare was turned into a major issue by the newspapers.

Submarine warfare was a phony issue. Germany and England were at war. Each was blockading the other country. J. P. Morgan and other financiers were selling munitions to Britain. The Germans could not allow those supplies to be delivered any more than the English would have allowed them to be delivered to Germany. If Morgan wanted to take the risks and reap the rewards (or suffer the consequences) of selling munitions to England, that was his business. It was certainly nothing over which the entire nation should have been dragged into war.

The Lusitania, at the time it was sunk, was carrying six million pounds of ammunition. It was actually illegal for American passengers to be aboard a ship carrying munitions to belligerents. Almost two years before the liner was sunk, the *New York Tribune* (June 19, 1913) carried a squib which stated: "Cunard officials acknowledged to the *Tribune* correspondent today that the greyhound [Lusitania] is being equipped with high power naval rifles. . . ." In fact, the Lusitania was registered in the British navy as an auxiliary cruiser. (Barnes, Harry E., *The Genesis of the War*, Alfred Knopf, New York, 1926, p. 611.) In addition, the German government took out large ads in all the New York papers warning potential passengers that the ship was carrying munitions and telling them not to cross the Atlantic on it. Those who chose to make the trip knew the risk they were taking. Yet the sink-

"Colonel" House (l) was front man for the international banking fraternity. He manipulated President Woodrow Wilson (r) like a puppet. Wilson called him "my alter ego." House played a major role in creating the Federal Reserve System, passing the graduated income tax and getting America into WWI. House's influence over Wilson is an example that in the world of super-politics the real rulers are not always the ones the public sees.

German born international financier Paul Warburg masterminded establishment of Federal Reserve to put control over nation's economy in hands of international bankers. The Federal Reserve controls the money supply which allows manipulators to create alternate cycles of boom and bust, i.e., a roller coaster economy. This allows those in the know to make fabulous amounts of money, but even more important, allows the **Insiders** to control the economy and further centralize power in the federal government.

ing of the Lusitania was used by clever propagandists to portray the Germans as inhuman slaughterers of innocents. Submarine warfare was manufactured into a *cause celebre* to push us into war. On April 6, 1917, Congress declared war. The American people acquiesced on the basis that it would be a "war to end all wars."

During the "war to end all wars," *Insider* banker Bernard Baruch was made absolute dictator over American business when President Wilson appointed him Chairman of the War Industries Board, where he had control of all domestic contracts for Allied war materials. Baruch made lots of friends while placing tens of billions in government contracts, and it was widely rumored in Wall Street that out of the war to make the world safe for international bankers he netted $200 million for himself.⑤

While *Insider* banker Paul Warburg controlled the Federal Reserve, and international banker Bernard Baruch placed government contracts, international banker Eugene Meyer, a former partner of Baruch and the son of a partner in the Rothschilds' international banking house of Lazard Freres, was Wilson's choice to head the War Finance Corporation, where he too made a little money*.

It should be noted that Sir William Wiseman, the man sent by British Intelligence to help bring the United States into the war, was amply rewarded for his services. He stayed in this country after WWI as a new partner in the Jacob Schiff-Paul Warburg-controlled Kuhn, Loeb bank.⑥

World War I was a financial bonanza for the international bankers. But it was a catastrophe of such magnitude for the United States that few even today grasp its importance. The war reversed our traditional foreign policy of non-involvement and we have been enmeshed almost constantly ever since in perpetual wars for perpetual peace. Winston Churchill once observed that all nations would have been better off had the U. S. minded its own business. Had we done so, he said, "peace would have been made with Germany; and there would have

(*Meyer later gained control of the highly influential *Washington Post* which became known as the "*Washington Daily Worker*.")   75

been no collapse in Russia leading to Communism; no breakdown of government in Italy followed by Fascism; and Naziism never would have gained ascendancy in Germany." (*Social Justice* Magazine, July 3, 1939, p. 4.)

The Bolshevik Revolution in Russia was obviously one of the great turning points in world history. It is an event over which misinformation abounds. The myth-makers and rewriters of history have done their landscape painting jobs well. The establishing of Communism in Russia is a classic example of the second "big lie" of Communism, i.e., that it is the movement of the downtrodden masses rising up against exploiting bosses. This cunning deception has been fostered since before the first French Revolution in 1789.

Most people today believe the Communists were successful in Russia because they were able to rally behind them the sympathy and frustration of the Russian people who were sick of the tyranny of the Czars. This is to ignore the history of what actually happened. While almost everybody is reminded that the Bolshevik Revolution took place in November of 1917, few know that the Czar had abdicated seven months earlier in March.⑦ When Czar Nicholas II abdicated, a provisional government was established by Prince Lvov who wanted to pattern the new Russian government after our own. But, unfortunately, the Lvov government gave way to the Kerensky regime. Kerensky, a so-called democratic socialist, may have been running a caretaker government for the Communists. He kept the war going against Germany and the other Central Powers, but he issued a general amnesty for Communists and other revolutionaries, many of whom had been exiled after the abortive Red Revolution of 1905. Back to mother Russia came 250,000 dedicated revolutionaries, and Kerensky's own government's doom was sealed.⑧

In the Soviet Union, as in every Communist country (or as they call themselves—the Socialist countries), the power has not come to the Communists' hands because the downtrodden masses willed it so. The power has come *from the top down* in every instance. Let us briefly reconstruct the sequences of the Communist takeover.

The year is 1917. The Allies are fighting the Central Powers. The Allies include Russia, the British Commonwealth, France and by April 1917, the United States. In March of 1917, purposeful planners set in motion the forces to compel Czar Nicholas II to abdicate. He did so under pressure from the Allies after severe riots in the Czarist capitol of Petrograd, riots that were caused by the breakdowns in the transportation system which cut the city off from food supplies and led to the closing of factories.⑨

But where were Lenin and Trotsky when all this was taking place? Lenin was in Switzerland and had been in Western Europe since 1905 when he was exiled for trying to topple the Czar in the abortive Communist revolution of that year. Trotsky also was in exile, a reporter for a Communist newspaper on the lower east side of New York City.⑩ The Bolsheviks were not a visible political force at the time the Czar abdicated. And they came to power not because the downtrodden masses of Russia called them *back*, but because very powerful men in Europe and the United States *sent them in.*⑪

Lenin was sent across Europe-at-war on the famous "sealed train." With him Lenin took some $5 to $6 million in gold. The whole thing was arranged by the German high command and Max Warburg, through another very wealthy and life-long socialist by the name of Alexander Helphand alias "Parvus." When Trotsky left New York aboard the S. S. Christiania, on March 27, 1917, with his entourage of 275 revolutionaries, the first port of call was Halifax, Nova Scotia. There the Canadians grabbed Trotsky and his money and impounded them both. This was a very logical thing for the Canadian government to do for Trotsky had said many times that if he were successful in coming to power in Russia he would immediately stop what he called the "imperialist war" and sue for a separate peace with Germany. This would free millions of German troops for transfer from the Eastern front to the Western front where they could kill Canadians. So Trotsky cooled his heels in a Canadian prison—for five days. Then all of a sudden the British (through future Kuhn, Loeb partner Sir William Wiseman) and the United States (through none other than the ubiquitous "Colonel" House) pressured the Canadian government. And, despite the fact we were now in the war, said, in so many words, "Let Trotsky go." Thus, with an American passport, Trotsky went back to meet Lenin.[12] They joined up, and, by November, through bribery, cunning, brutality and deception, they were able (not to bring the masses rallying to their cause, but) to hire enough thugs and make enough deals to impose out of the gun barrel what Lenin called "all power to the Soviets." The Communists came to power by seizing a mere handful of key cities. In fact, practically the whole Bolshevik Revolution took place in one city —Petrograd. It was as if the whole United States became Communist because a Communist-led mob seized Washington, D. C. It was years before the Soviets solidified power throughout Russia.[13]

The Germans, on the face of it, had a plausible excuse for financing Lenin and Trotsky. The two Germans most responsible for the financing of Lenin were Max Warburg and a displaced Russian named Alexander Helphand. They could claim that they were serving their country's cause by helping and financing Lenin. However, these two German "patriots" neglected to mention to the Kaiser their plan to foment a Communist revolution in Russia.[14] The picture takes on another dimension when you consider that the brother of Max Warburg was Paul Warburg, prime mover in establishing the Federal Reserve System and who from his position on the Federal Reserve Board of Directors, played a key role in financing the American war effort. (When news leaked out in American papers about brother Max running the German finances, Paul resigned from his Federal Reserve post without a whimper.) From here on the plot sickens.

For the father-in-law of Max Warburg's brother, Felix,

was Jacob Schiff, senior partner in Kuhn, Loeb & Co. (Paul and Felix Warburg, you will recall, were also partners in Kuhn, Loeb & Co. while Max ran the Rothschild-allied family bank of Frankfurt.) Jacob Schiff also helped finance Leon Trotsky. According to the *New York Journal-American* of February 3, 1949: "Today it is estimated by Jacob's grandson, John Schiff, that the old man sank about 20,000,000 dollars for the final triumph of Bolshevism in Russia." (See Chart 6.)

One of the best sources of information on the financing of the Bolshevik Revolution is *Czarism and the Revolution* by an important White Russian General named Arsene de Goulevitch who was founder in France of the Union of Oppressed Peoples. In this volume, written in French and subsequently translated into English, de Goulevitch notes:

> "The main purveyors of funds for the revolution, however, were neither the crackpot Russian millionaires nor the armed bandits of Lenin. The 'real' money primarily came from certain British and American circles which for a long time past had lent their support to the Russian revolutionary cause. . . .⑮

De Goulevitch continues:

> "The important part played by the wealthy American banker, Jacob Schiff, in the events in Russia, though as yet only partially revealed, is no longer a secret."

General Alexander Nechvolodov is quoted by de Goulevitch as stating in his book on the Bolshevik Revolution:

> "In April 1917, Jacob Schiff publicly declared that it was thanks to his financial support that the revolution in Russia had succeeded.
> In the Spring of the same year, Schiff commenced

79

to subsidize Trotsky . . .

Simultaneously Trotsky and Co. were also being subsidized by Max Warburg and Olaf Aschberg of the Nye Banken of Stockholm . . . The Rhine Westphalian Syndicate and Jivotovsky, . . . whose daughter later married Trotsky."

Schiff spent millions to overthrow the Czar and more millions to overthrow Kerensky. He was sending money to Russia long after the true character of the Bolsheviks was known to the world. Schiff raised $10 million, supposedly for Jewish war relief in Russia, but later events revealed it to be a good business investment.[16]

According to de Goulevitch:

"Mr. Bakhmetiev, the late Russian Imperial Ambassador to the United States, tells us that the Bol-

FINANCING
BOLSHEVIK REVOLUTION

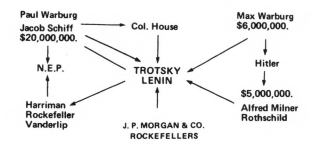

sheviks, after victory, transferred 600 million roubles in gold between the years 1918 and 1922 to Kuhn, Loeb & Company [Schiff's firm].[17]

Schiff's participation in the Bolshevik Revolution, though quite naturally now denied, was well known among Allied intelligence services at the time. This led to much talk about Bolshevism being a Jewish plot. The result was that the subject of financing the Communist takeover of Russia became taboo. Later evidence indicates that the bankrolling of the Bolsheviks was handled by a syndicate of international bankers, which in addition to the Schiff-Warburg clique, included Morgan and Rockefeller interests. Documents show that the Morgan organization put at least $1 million in the Red revolutionary kitty.[18]

Still another important financier of the Bolshevik Revolution was an extremely wealthy Englishman named Lord Alfred Milner, the organizer and head of a secret organization called "The Round Table" Group which was backed by Lord Rothschild (discussed in the next chapter).

De Goulevitch notes further:

> "On April 7, 1917, General Janin made the following entry in his diary ('Au G.C.C. Russé'—At Russian G.H.Q.—Le Monde Slave, Vol. 2, 1927, pp. 296-297): Long interview with R., who confirmed what I had previously been told by M. After referring to the German hatred of himself and his family, he turned to the subject of the Revolution which, he claimed, was engineered by the English, more precisely, by Sir George Buchanan and Lord [Alfred] Milner. Petrograd at the time was teeming with English. . . . He could, he asserted, name the streets and the numbers of the houses in which British agents were quartered. They were reported, during the rising, to have distributed money

to the soldiers and incited them to mutiny."[19]

De Goulevitch goes on to reveal: "In private interviews I have been told that over 21 million roubles were spent by Lord Milner in financing the Russian Revolution."

It should be noted parenthetically that Lord Milner, Paul, Felix and Max Warburg represented "their" respective countries at the Paris Peace Conference at the conclusion of World War I.

If we can somehow ascribe Max Warburg's financing of Lenin to German "patriotism," it was certainly not patriotism" which inspired Schiff, Morgan, Rockefeller and Milner to bankroll the Bolsheviks. Both Britain and America were at war with Germany and were allies of Czarist Russia. To free dozens of German divisions to switch from the Eastern front to France and kill hundreds of thousands of American and British soldiers was nothing short of treason.[20]

In the Bolshevik Revolution we see many of the same old faces that were responsible for creating the Federal Reserve System, initiating the graduated income tax, setting up the tax-free foundations and pushing us into WWI. However, if you conclude that this is anything but coincidental, your name will be immediately expunged from the Social Register.

No revolution can be successful without organization and money. "The downtrodden masses" usually provide little of the former and none of the latter. But *Insiders* at the top can arrange for both.

What did these people possibly have to gain in financing the Russian Revolution? What did they have to gain by keeping it alive and afloat, or, during the 1920's by pouring millions of dollars into what Lenin called his New Economic Program, thus saving the Soviets from collapse?

Why would these "capitalists" do all this? If your goal is global conquest, you have to start somewhere. It may or may not have been coincidental, but Russia was the one major European country without a central bank. In Russia, for the

Lord Alfred Milner, wealthy Englishman and front man for the Rothschilds, served as paymaster for the international bankers in Petrograd during the Bolshevik Revolution. Milner later headed secret society known as The Round Table which was dedicated to establishing a world government whereby a clique of super-rich financiers would control the world under the guise of Socialism. The American subsidiary of this conspiracy is called the Council on Foreign Relations and was started by, and is still controlled by Leftist international bankers.

According to his grandson John, Jacob Schiff (above), long-time associate of the Rothschilds, financed the Communist Revolution in Russia to the tune of $20 million. According to a report on file with the State Department, his firm, Kuhn Loeb and Co. bankrolled the first five year plan for Stalin. Schiff's partner and relative, Paul Warburg, engineered the establishment of the Federal Reserve System while on the Kuhn Loeb payroll. Schiff's descendants are active in the Council on Foreign Relations today.

Home of the Council on Foreign Relations on 68th St. in New York. The admitted goal of the CFR is to abolish the Constitution and replace our once independent Republic with a World Government. CFR members have controlled the last six administrations. Richard Nixon has been a member and has appointed at least 100 CFR members to high positions in his administration.

first time, the Communist conspiracy gained a geographical homeland from which to launch assaults against the other nations of the world. The West now had an enemy.

In the Bolshevik Revolution we have some of the world's richest and most powerful men financing a movement which claims its very existence is based on the concept of stripping of their wealth men like the Rothschilds, Rockefellers, Schiffs, Warburgs, Morgans, Harrimans, and Milners. But obviously these men have no fear of international Communism. It is only logical to assume that if they financed it and do not fear it, it must be because they control it. Can there be any other explanation that makes sense? Remember that for over 150 years it has been standard operating procedure of the Rothschilds and their allies to control both sides of every conflict. You must have an "enemy" if you are going to collect from the King. The East-West balance-of-power politics is used as one of the main excuses for the socialization of America. Although it was not their main purpose, by nationalization of Russia the *Insiders* bought themselves an enormous piece of real estate, complete with mineral rights, for somewhere between $30 and $40 million.

We can only theorize on the manner in which Moscow is controlled from New York, London and Paris. Undoubtedly much of the control is economic, but certainly the international bankers have an enforcer arm within Russia to keep the Soviet leaders in line. The organization may be SMERSH, the international Communist murder organization described in testimony before Congressional Committees and by Ian Fleming in his James Bond books. For although the Bond novels were wildly imaginative, Fleming had been in British Navy intelligence, maintained excellent intelligence contacts around the world and was reputedly a keen student of the international conspiracy.[21]

We do know this, however. A clique of American financiers not only helped establish Communism in Russia, but has striven mightily ever since to keep it alive. Ever since 1918 this clique has been engaged in transferring money and, probably more important, technical information, to the Soviet Union. This is made abundantly clear in the three volume history *Western Technology and Soviet Economic Development* by scholar Antony Sutton of Stanford University's Hoover Institution on War, Revolution and Peace. Using, for the most part, official State Department documents, Sutton shows conclusively that virtually everything the Soviets possess has been acquired from the West. It is not much of an exaggeration to say that the U.S.S.R. was made in the U.S.A. The landscape painters, unable to refute Sutton's monumental scholarship, simply paint him out of the picture.

At Versailles, this same clique carved up Europe and set the stage for World War II. As Lord Curzon commented: "It is not a peace treaty, it is simply a break in hostilities." In 1933, the same *Insiders* pushed FDR into recognizing the Soviet Union, thus saving it from financial collapse, while at the same time they were underwriting huge loans on both sides of the Atlantic for the new regime of Adolph Hitler. In so doing they assisted greatly in setting the stage for World War II, and the events that followed. In 1941, the same *Insiders* rushed to the aid of our "noble ally," Stalin, after his break with Hitler. In 1943, these same *Insiders* marched off to the Teheran Conference and proceeded to start the carving up of Europe after the second great "war to end war." Again at Yalta and Potsdam in 1945, they established the China policy . . . later summarized by Owen Lattimore: "The problem was how to allow them [China] to fall without making it look as if the United States had pushed them." The facts are inescapable. In one country after another Communism has been imposed on the local population from the top down. The most prominent forces for the imposition of that tyranny came from the United States and Great Britain. Here is a charge that no American enjoys making, but the facts lead to no other possible conclusion. The idea that Communism is a movement of the downtrodden masses is a fraud.

None of the foregoing makes sense if Communism really is what the Communists and the Establishment tell us it is. But if Communism is an arm of a bigger conspiracy to control the world by power-mad billionaires (and brilliant but ruthless academicians who have shown them how to use their power) it all becomes perfectly logical.

It is at this point that we should again make it clear that this conspiracy is not made up solely of bankers and international cartelists, but includes every field of human endeavor. Starting with Voltaire and Adam Weishaupt and running through John Ruskin, Sidney Webb, Nicholas Murray Butler, and on to the present Henry Kissinger and John Kenneth Galbraith, it has always been the scholar looking for avenues of power who has shown the "sons of the very powerful" how their wealth could be used to rule the world.

We cannot stress too greatly the importance of the reader keeping in mind that this book is discussing only one segment of the conspiracy, certain international bankers. Other equally important segments which work to foment labor, religious and racial strife in order to promote socialism have been described in numerous other books. These other divisions of the conspiracy operate independently of the international bankers in most cases and it would certainly be disastrous to ignore the danger to our freedom they represent.[22]

It would be equally disastrous to lump all businessmen and bankers into the conspiracy. One must draw the distinction between competitive free enterprise, the most moral and productive system ever devised, and cartel capitalism dominated by industrial monopolists and international bankers. The difference is the private enterpriser operates by offering products and services in a competitive free market while the cartel capitalist uses the government to force the public to do business with him. These corporate socialists are deadly enemies of competitive private enterprise.

Liberals are willing to believe that these "robber barons" will fix prices, rig markets, establish monopolies, buy politicians, exploit employees and fire them the day before they are eligible for pensions, but they absolutely will not believe that these same men would want to rule the world or would use Communism as the striking edge of their conspiracy. When one discusses the machinations of these men, Liberals usually respond by saying, "But don't you think they mean well?"

However, if you think with logic, reason and precision in this field and try to expose these power seekers, the Establishment's mass media will accuse you of being a dangerous paranoid who is "dividing" our people. In every other area, of course, they encourage dissent as being healthy in a "democracy."

Chapter V

Establishing the Establishment

One of the primary reasons the *Insiders* worked behind the scenes to foment WWI was to create in its aftermath a world government. If you wish to establish national monopolies, you must control national governments. If you wish to establish international monopolies or cartels, you must control a world government.

After the Armistice on November 11, 1918, Woodrow Wilson and his *alter ego*, "Colonel" House (the ever present front man for the *Insiders*), went to Europe in hopes of establishing a world government in the form of the League of Nations. When the negotiations revealed one side had been about as guilty as the other, and the glitter of the "moral crusade" evaporated along with Wilson's vaunted "Fourteen Points," the "rubes back on Main Street" began to waken. Reaction and disillusionment set in.

Americans certainly didn't want to get into a World Government with double-dealing Europeans whose specialty was secret treaty hidden behind secret treaty. The guest of honor, so to speak, stalked out of the banquet before the poisoned meal could be served. And, without American inclusion, there could be no meaningful World Government.

Aroused public opinion made it obvious that the U. S. Senate dared not ratify a treaty saddling the country with such an international commitment. In some manner the American public had been sold on the idea of internationalism and World Government. Again, the key was "Colonel" House.

House had set down his political ideas in his book called *Philip Dru: Administrator* in 1912. In this book House laid out a thinly fictionalized plan for conquest of America by establishing "Socialism as dreamed by Karl Marx."[1] He described a "conspiracy"—the word is his—which succeeds in electing a U. S. President by means of "deception regarding his real opinions and intentions." Among other things, House wrote that the conspiracy was to insinuate "itself into the primaries, in order that no candidate might be nominated whose views were not in accord with theirs." Elections were to become mere charades conducted for the bedazzlement of the booboisie. The idea was to use both the Democrat and Republican parties as instruments to promote World Government.

In 1919 House met in Paris with members of a British "secret society" called The Round Table in order to form an organization whose job it would be to propagandize the citizens of America, England and Western Europe on the glories of World Government. The big selling point, of course, was "peace." The part about the *Insiders* establishing a world dictatorship quite naturally was left out.

The Round Table organization in England grew out of the life-long dream of gold and diamond magnate Cecil Rhodes for a "new world order."

Rhodes' biographer Sara Millin was a little more direct. As she put it: "The government of the world was Rhodes' simple desire."[2] Quigley quotes:

> "In the middle 1890's Rhodes had a personal income of at least a million pounds sterling a year (then about five million dollars) which he spent so freely for his mysterious purposes that he was usually

overdrawn on his account. . . ."③

Cecil Rhodes' commitment to a conspiracy to establish World Government was set down in a series of wills described by Frank Aydelotte in his book *American Rhodes Scholarships*. Aydelotte writes:

"The seven wills which Cecil Rhodes made between the ages of 24 and 46 [Rhodes died at age forty-eight] constitute a kind of spiritual autobiography. . . . Best known are the first (the Secret Society Will . . .), and the last, which established the Rhodes Scholarships. . . .

In his first will Rhodes states his aim still more specifically: 'The extension of British rule throughout the world. . . . the foundation of so great a power as to hereafter render wars impossible and promote the interests of humanity.'

The 'Confession of Faith' enlarges upon these ideas. The model for this proposed secret society was the Society of Jesus, though he mentions also the Masons."④

It should be noted that the originator of this type of secret society was Adam Weishaupt, the monster who founded the Order of Illuminati on May 1, 1776, for the purpose of conspiracy to control the world. The role of Weishaupt's Illuminists in such horrors as the Reign of Terror is unquestioned, and the techniques of the Illuminati have long been recognized as models for Communist methodology. Weishaupt also used the structure of the Society of Jesus (the Jesuits) as his model, and rewrote his Code in Masonic terms. Aydelotte continues:

"In 1888 Rhodes made his third will . . . leaving everything to Lord Rothschild [his financier in mining enterprises], with an accompanying letter enclosing 'the written matter discussed between us.' This, one surmises, consisted of the first will and the 'Confession of Faith,' since in a postscript Rhodes says 'in considering questions suggested take Constitution of the Jesuits if obtainable. . . .' "

Apparently for strategic reasons Lord Rothschild was subsequently removed from the forefront of the scheme. Professor Quigley reveals that Lord Rosebury "replaced his father-in-law Lord Rothschild, in Rhodes' next (and last), will."

The "secret society" was organized on the conspiratorial pattern of circles within circles. Professor Quigley informs us that the central part of the "secret society" was established by March, 1891, using Rhodes' money. The organization was run for Rothschild by Lord Alfred Milner, discussed in the last chapter as a key financier of the Bolshevik revolution. The Round Table worked behind the scenes at the highest levels of British government, influencing foreign policy and England's involvement and conduct of WWI. According to Professor Quigley:

"At the end of the war of 1914, it became clear that the organization of this system [the Round Table Group] had to be greatly extended. Once again the task was entrusted to Lionel Curtis who established, in England and each dominion, a front organization to the existing Round Table Group. This front organization, called the Royal Institute of International Affairs, had as its nucleus in each area the existing submerged Round Table Group. In New York it was known as the Council on Foreign Relations, and was a front for J. P. Morgan and Company in association with the very small American Round Table Group. The American organizers were dominated by the large number of Morgan 'experts,'

... who had gone to the Paris Peace Conference and there became close friends with the similar group of English 'experts' which had been recruited by the Milner group. In fact, the original plans for the Royal Institute of International Affairs and the Council on Foreign Relations [C.F.R.] were drawn up in Paris. . . ."⑤

Joseph Kraft (C.F.R.), however, tells us in *Harper's* of July 1958, that the chief agent in the formal founding of the Council on Foreign Relations was "Colonel" House, *supported* by such protegés as Walter Lippmann, John Foster Dulles, Allen Dulles and Christian Herter. It was House who acted as host for the Round Table Group, both English and American, at the key meeting of May 19, 1949, in the Majestic Hotel, Paris, which committed the conspiracy to creation of the C.F.R.

Although Quigley stresses the importance of Morgan men at the creation of the organization known as the Council on Foreign Relations, this organization's own materials and "Colonel" House's own memoirs reveal his function as midwife at the birth of the C.F.R.

The C.F.R.'s Twenty-Fifth Annual Report tells us this of the C.F.R.'s founding at Paris:

". . . The Institute of International Affairs founded at Paris in 1919 was comprised, at the outset, of two branches, one in the United Kingdom and one in the U.S. . . ."

Later the plan was changed to create an ostensible autonomy because, ". . . it seemed unwise to set up a single institute with branches." It had to be made to appear that the C.F.R. in America, and the R.I.I.A. in Britain, were really independent bodies, lest the American public become aware the C.F.R. was in fact a subsidiary of the Round Table Group and react in patriotic fury.

According to Quigley, the most important financial dynasties in America following WWI were (in addition to Morgan) the Rockefeller family; Kuhn, Loeb & Company; Dillon Read and Company and Brown Bros. Harriman.[6] All were represented in the C.F.R. and Paul Warburg was one of the incorporators. The *Insider* crowd which created the Federal Reserve System, many of whom also bankrolled the Bolshevik Revolution, were all in the original membership. In addition to Paul Warburg, founders of the C.F.R. included international financial *Insiders* Jacob Schiff, Averell Harriman, Frank Vanderlip, Nelson Aldrich, Bernard Baruch, J. P. Morgan and John D. Rockefeller. These men did not create the C.F.R. because they had nothing better to do with their time and money. They created it as a tool to further their ambitions.

The C.F.R. has come to be known as "The Establishment," "the invisible government" and "the Rockefeller foreign office." This semi-secret organization unquestionably has become the most influential group in America.

One of the extremely infrequent articles to appear in the national press concerning this Council was published in the *Christian Science Monitor* of September 1, 1961. It began this way:

> "On the west side of fashionable Park Avenue at 68th Street [in New York City] sit two handsome buildings across the way from each other. One is the Soviet Embassy to the United Nations. . . . Directly opposite on the southwest corner is the Council on Foreign Relations—probably one of the most influential semi-public organizations in the field of foreign policy."

Although the formal membership in the C.F.R. is composed of close to 1500 of the most elite names in the worlds of government, labor, business, finance, communications, the foundations, and the academy—and despite the fact that it has staffed almost every key position of every administration since those of FDR—it is doubtful that one American in a thousand so much as recognized the Council's name, or that one in ten thousand can relate anything at all about its structure or purpose. Indicative of the C.F.R.'s power to maintain its anonymity is the fact that, despite its having been operative at the highest levels for nearly fifty years and having from the beginning counted among its members the foremost lions of the Establishment communications media, we discovered after poring over volumes of the *Reader's Guide To Periodical Literature* covering several decades that only one magazine article on the C.F.R. has ever appeared in a major national journal—and that in *Harper's*, hardly a mass-circulation periodical. Similarly, only a handful of articles on the Council have appeared in the nation's great newspapers. Such anonymity—at that level—can hardly be a matter of mere chance.

What makes this secret organization so influential? No one who knows for a certainty will say. The *Christian Science Monitor*, which is edited by a member of the American Round Table (a branch of Milner's secret society) did not in the article of September 1, 1961, that "its roster . . . contains names distinguished in the field of diplomacy, government, business, finance, science, labor, journalism, law and education. What united so wide-ranging and disparate a membership is a passionate concern for the direction of American foreign policy."

The *Christian Science Monitor* indicates the fantastic power the C.F.R. has had during the last six administrations:

> "Because of the Council's single-minded dedication to studying and deliberating American foreign policy, there is a constant flow of its members from private to public service. *Almost half of the Council members have been invited to assume official government positions or to act as consultants at one time or*

another." [Emphasis added]

The policies promoted by the C.F.R. in the fields of defense and international relations become, with a regularity which defies the laws of chance, the official policies of the United States Government. As Liberal columnist Joseph Kraft, himself a member of the C.F.R., noted of the Council in the *Harper's* article: "It has been the seat of some basic government decisions, has set the context for many more, and has repeatedly served as a recruiting ground for ranking officials." Kraft, incidentally, aptly titled his article on the C.F.R., "School for Statesmen"—an admission that the members of the Council are drilled with a "line" of strategy to be carried out in Washington.

As World War II approached, the Round Table Group was influential in seeing that Hitler was not stopped in Austria, the Rhineland, or Sudetenland—and thereby was largely responsible for precipitating the holocaust. A second world war would greatly enhance the opportunity for establishment of World Government. The financing for Adolph Hitler's rise to power was handled through the Warburg-controlled Mendelsohn Bank of Amsterdam and later by the J. Henry Schroeder Bank with branches in Frankfurt, London and New York. Chief legal counsel to the J. Henry Schroeder Bank was the firm of Sullivan and Cromwell whose senior partners included John Foster and Allen Dulles, (See James Martin's *All Honorable Men*, Little Brown Co., New York, 1950, p. 51. See also Quigley, p. 433.)

With the Round Table doing its work in Europe, the C.F.R. carried the ball in the United States. The Council's first task was to infiltrate and develop effective control of the U.S. State Department—to make certain that after World War II there would be no slip-ups as there had been following World War I. The story of the C.F.R. takeover of the Department of State is contained in State Department Publication 2349, *Report To The President On The Results of the San Fran-*

cisco Conference. It is the report of Secretary of State Edward R. Stettinius (C.F.R.) to President Truman. On page twenty we find:

> "With the outbreak of war in Europe it was clear that the United States would be confronted, after the war, with new and exceptional problems. . . . Accordingly, a Committee on Post-War Problems was set up before the end of 1939 [two years before the U.S. entered the war], at the suggestion of the C.F.R. The Committee consisted of high officials of the Department of State [all but one of whom were C.F.R. members]. It was assisted by a research staff [provided by, financed by, and directed by the C.F.R.], which in February, 1941, was organized into a Division of Special Research [and went off the C.F.R. payroll and onto that of the State Department].
>
> [After Pearl Harbor] the research facilities were rapidly expanded, and the Departmental Committee on Post-War Problems was reorganized into an Advisory Committee on Post-War Foreign Policies [completely staffed by the C.F.R.]." (See also the C.F.R.'s booklet, *A Record of Twenty Years, 1921-1947.*)

This is the group which designed the United Nations—the first major successful step on the road to a World Superstate. At least forty-seven C.F.R. members were among the American delegates to the founding of the United Nations in San Francisco in 1945. Members of the C.F.R. group included Harold Stassen, John J. McCloy, Owen Lattimore (called by the Senate Internal Security Subcommittee a "conscious articulate instrument of the Soviet conspiracy"), Alger Hiss (Communist spy), Philip Jessup, Harry Dexter White (Communist agent), Nelson Rockefeller, John Foster Dulles, John Carter Vincent (security risk), and Dean Acheson. Just to make sure that Communist Party members understood the importance of the U.N. establishment, *Political Affairs*, the Party's official theoretical journal, in the April 1945 issue, gave the order:

"Great popular support and enthusiasm for the United Nations policies should be built up, well organized and fully articulate. But it is also necessary to do more than that. The opposition must be rendered so impotent that it will be unable to gather any significant support in the Senate against the United Nations Charter and the treaties which will follow."

One wonders if the boobs at the Party level ever questioned why they were to support an organization dominated by the hated "Wall Street" personalities. The landscape painters of the mass media have outdone themselves painting the U. N. as a peace organization instead of a front for the international bankers.

Not only did members of the Council on Foreign Relations dominate the establishment of the U.N., but C.F.R. members were at the elbow of the American President at Teheran, Potsdam and Yalta—where hundreds of millions of human beings were delivered into the hands of Joseph Stalin, vastly extending the power of the International Communist Conspiracy. Administrative assistant to FDR during this time was a key member of the C.F.R. named Lauchlin Currie—subsequently identified by J. Edgar Hoover as a Soviet agent.

So completely has the C.F.R. dominated the State Department over the past thirty-eight years that every Secretary of State except Cordell Hull, James Byrnes, and William Rogers has been a member of the C.F.R. While Rogers is not a member, Professor Henry Kissinger, Mr. Nixon's chief foreign policy advisor, came to the job from the staff of the C.F.R., and the undersecretaries of state, almost to a man, are C.F.R members.

Today the C.F.R. remains active in working toward its final goal of a government over all the world—a government which the *Insiders* and their allies will control. The goal of the C.F.R. is simply to abolish the United States with its Constitutional guarantees of liberty. And they don't even try to hide it. *Study No.* 7, published by the C.F.R. on November 25, 1959, openly advocates "building a new international order [which] must be responsive to world aspirations for peace, [and] for social and economic change . . . an international order [code word for world government] . . . including states labeling themselves as 'Socialist' [Communist]."⑦

The reason is evident to those who have studied its membership for this little known semi-secret organization to be called "the Establishment." (See Chart 7) International banking organizations that currently have men in the C.F.R. include Kuhn, Loeb & Company; Lazard Freres (directly affiliated with Rothschild); Dillon Read; Lehman Bros.; Goldman, Sachs; Chase Manhattan Bank; Morgan Guaranty Bank; Brown Bros. Harriman; First National City Bank; Chemical Bank & Trust, and Manufacturers Hanover Trust Bank.⑧

Among the major corporations that have men in the C.F.R. are Standard Oil, IBM, Xerox, Eastman Kodak, Pan American, Firestone, U. S. Steel, General Electric and American Telephone and Telegraph Company.

Also in the C.F.R. are men from such openly Leftist organizations as the Fabian Socialist Americans for Democratic Action, the avowedly Socialist League for Industrial Democracy —(formerly the Intercollegiate Socialist Society), and the United World Federalists which openly advocates world government with the Communists. Such devotedly Socialist labor leaders as the late Walter Reuther, David Dubinsky and Jay Lovestone have also been members of the C.F.R. In theory, these men and organizations are supposed to be the blood enemies of the banks and businesses listed above. Yet they all belong to the same lodge. You can see why that fact is not advertised.

WORLD SUPRA-GOVERNMENT

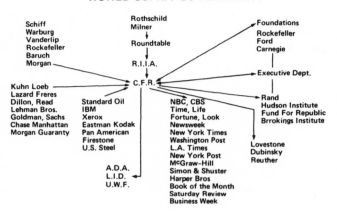

The C.F.R. is totally interlocked with the major foundations and so-called "Think Tanks." Included in the interlock are the Rockefeller, Ford and Carnegie foundations and the Rand Corporation, Hudson Institute, Fund for the Republic and Brookings Institute "Think Tanks."

The fact that the C.F.R. operates in near-complete anonymity can hardly be accidental. Among the communications corporations represented in the C.F.R. are National Broadcasting Corporation, Columbia Broadcasting System, *Time, Life, Fortune, Look, Newsweek, New York Times, Washington Post, Los Angeles Times, New York Post, Denver Post, Louisville Courier Journal, Minneapolis Tribune,* the Knight papers, McGraw-Hill, Simon & Schuster, Harper Bros., Random House, Little Brown & Co., Macmillan Co., Viking Press, *Saturday Review, Business Week* and Book of the Month Club. Surely the C.F.R. could get a few blurbs of publicity if publicity were desired. If it seems impossible that one entity could control such a vast array of firms, it is because most people do not know that the so-called founders of such giants as the *New York Times* and NBC were chosen, financed and directed by Morgan, Schiff and their allies. The case of Adolph Ochs of the *Times* and David Sarnoff of RCA are examples of this control. Both were given early financial aid by Kuhn, Loeb & Company and Morgan Guaranty.

These are the Establishment's official landscape painters whose jobs it is to make sure the public does not discover the C.F.R. and its role in creating a world socialist dictatorship.

You will recall that "Colonel" House believed we should have two political parties but only a single ideology—One World Socialism. This is exactly what we have in this country today. (See Chart 8) Although there are philosophical differences between the grass roots Democrats and the grass roots Republicans, yet as you move up the party ladders these differences become less and less distinguishable until finally the ladders disappear behind the Establishment's managed news curtain and come together at the apex under the control of the C.F.R. In 1968, when George Wallace maintained that there wasn't a dime's worth of difference between the two parties, he may not have known how right he was or why.

The following so-called Democrats who have been or now are C.F.R. agents: Dean Acheson, Alger Hiss, Adlai Stevenson, John Kennedy, Robert Kennedy, Edward Kennedy,* Averell Harriman, George Ball, Henry Fowler, Dean Rusk, Adam Yarmolinsky, Hubert Humphrey and John Lindsay.

It is interesting to note that rewards of cushy jobs were given by the international bankers to many men high in the LBJ administration for their services. Undersecretary of State George Ball went with Lehman Brothers; Secretary of the Treasury Henry Fowler was taken in by Goldman, Sachs & Co.; Budget Director Peter Lewis, Undersecretary of the Treasury Frederick Deming and former Secretary of Commerce C. R. Smith all avoided the bread lines by being picked up by Lazard Freres (Rothschilds). Fowler and Deming were largely responsible for policies which led to European nations

101

CONTROL OF POLITICAL PARTIES

CFR

Managed News Curtain

Democrat   Republican

DEMOCRATS

DEAN ACHESON

ALGER HISS

ADLAI STEVENSON

JOHN KENNEDY

ROBERT KENNEDY

AVERILL HARRIMAN

GEORGE BALL

HENRY FOWLER

DEAN RUSK

ADAM YARMOLINSKY

JOHN K. GALBRAITH

ARTHUR SCHLESINGER, Jr.

JOHN LINDSAY

HUBERT HUMPHREY

REPUBLICANS

DWIGHT EISENHOWER

JOHN FOSTER DULLES

THOMAS E. DEWEY

JACOB JAVITS

PAUL HOFFMAN

ROBERT MacNAMARA

JOHN GARDNER

HENRY CABOT LODGE

ROCKEFELLERS

ELIOT RICHARDSON

ARTHUR BURNS

HENRY KISSINGER

RICHARD NIXON

claiming half of our gold (and having potential claims on the rest) as well as denuding the U. S. Treasury of all of the silver reserves it had built up over a century of time. Did the international bankers take pity on these men for their incompetence or were they rewarded for a job well done?

Controlling the Republican Party for the C.F.R. have been Dwight D. Eisenhower, John Foster Dulles, Thomas E. Dewey, Jacob Javits, Robert McNamara, Henry Cabot Lodge, Paul Hoffman, John Gardner, the Rockefeller clan, Elliott Richardson, Arthur Burns, Henry Kissinger and Richard Nixon.**

While it is true that every administration since FDR has been dominated by the C.F.R., the Nixon Administration has set the all-time record by appointing over 110 C.F.R. members to key positions. Henry Kissinger, the "Colonel" House of the Nixon Administration, came to his job directly from employment on the C.F.R. staff. Kissinger represents the very opposite of everything Nixon said he stood for in his campaign. Both Liberals and Conservatives admit Kissinger is by far the most important man in the Nixon Administration.

Administrations, both Democrat and Republican, come and go—but the C.F.R. lingers on. This is why the more things seem to change, the more they remain the same. The fix is in at the top, where the same coterie of *Insiders*, bent on control of the world, runs the show. As Professor Quigley admits:

> "There does exist, and has existed for a generation, an international . . . network which operates, to some extent, in the way the radical Right believes the Communists act. In fact, this network, which we may identify as the Round Table Groups, *has no aversion to cooperating with the Communists, or any other groups, and frequently does so.*" [Emphasis added.]⑨

Yes, the *Insiders* have no aversion to working with the Communists whose ostensible goal is to destroy them. While the

103

Insiders are serving champagne and caviar to their guests in their summer mansions at Newport, or entertaining other members of the social elite aboard their yachts, their agents are out enslaving and murdering people. And you are next on their list.

Clearly, the *Chicago Tribune's* editorial of December 9, 1950, on the C.F.R. still applies:

> "The members of the council [On Foreign Relations] are persons of much more than average influence in their community. They have used the prestige that their wealth, their social position, and their education have given them to lead their country toward bankruptcy and military debacle. They should look at their hands. There is blood on them—the dried blood of the last war and the fresh blood of the present one [the Korean War]."

It goes without saying that the C.F.R.'s hands are bloodier now with the gore of 50,000 Americans in Vietnam. Shamefully the Council has succeeded in promoting, as American policy, the shipment of American aid and trade to the East European arsenal of the Viet Cong for the killing of our sons in the field.

It should not be surprising to learn that there is on the international level an organization equivalent of the C.F.R. This group calls itself the Bilderbergers. If scarcely one American in a thousand has any familiarity with the C.F.R., it is doubtful that one in five thousand has any knowledge of the Bilderbergers. Again, this is not accidental.

The strange name of this group is taken from the site of the first meeting in May, 1954—the Hotel de Bilderberg—in Oostebeck, Holland. The man who created the Bilderbergers is His Royal Highness Prince Bernhard of the Netherlands. The Prince is an important figure in Royal Dutch Petroleum (Shell Oil) and the Societe General de Belgique, a huge conglomerate cartel with worldwide holdings. The Bilderbergers meet once—or sometimes twice—a year. Those in attendance include leading political and financial figures from the United States and Western Europe. Prince Bernhard makes no effort to hide the fact that the ultimate goal of the Bilderbergers is a world government. In the meantime, while the "new world order" is being built, the Bilderbergers coordinate the efforts of the European and American power elites.

Prince Bernhard's counterpart among the American Bilderbergers is David Rockefeller, chairman of the board of the C.F.R., whose economic base is the giant Chase Manhattan Bank and Standard Oil. Among the other Bilderbergers from the world of ultra-high finance are Baron Edmund de Rothschild of the House of Rothschild, C. Douglas Dillon (C.F.R.) of Dillon Read & Co., Robert McNamara of the World Bank, Sir Eric Roll of S. G. Warburg & Co., Ltd., Pierce Paul Schweitzer of the International Monetary Fund, and George Ball (C.F.R.) of Lehman Brothers.

Not everyone who attends one of the Bilderbergers' secret meetings is an *Insider*, but only men of the Left are allowed to attend the private meetings following the general sessions. The avowedly Socialist Parties of Europe are well represented . . . another example of the tie-in between the *Insiders* of high finance and the ostensible leaders of the proletariat. Bilderberg policy is not planned by those who attend the conferences, but by the elite steering committee of *Insiders* composed of 24 Europeans and 15 Americans. Past and present Americans 'of the Bilderberger Steering Committee include George W. Ball, Gardner Cowles, John H. Ferguson, Henry J. Heinz II, Robert D. Murphy, David Rockefeller, Shepard Stone, James D. Zellerbach, Emelio G. Collado, Arthur H. Dean, Gabriel Hauge, C. D. Jackson, George Nebolsine, Dean Rusk and General Walter Bedell Smith. Those who adhere to the accidental theory of history will claim that it is sheer coincidence that every single one of those named as past and present members of the Bilderberger Steering Committee is or was a member of the Council on Foreign Relations.

The Bilderberger Advisory Committee forms an even more "inner circle" than the Steering Committee. Americans on the Advisory Committee include Joseph E. Johnson, Dean Rusk, Arthur H. Dean, George Nebolsine, John S. Coleman, General Walter Bedell Smith and Henry J. Heinz II. Again, all are members of the C.F.R.

One would assume (that is, if one had not read this book) that when the world's leading parliamentarians and international tycoons meet to discuss the planning of their various nations' foreign policies, that the newshawks from papers and televisionland would be screaming to high heaven that such an event held in secret makes a mockery of the democratic process. One might expect Walter Cronkite to be thundering in wrath about an elite clique meeting to plan our lives; or the *New York Times* editorialists to be pounding their smoking typewriters, fuming about "the public's right to know." But, of course, the landscape painters merely brush the Bilderbergers right out of existence and focus the public's attention on something like the conditions in the prisons or coke bottles littering the highways. Since the Bilderbergers are a group of the Left (or, as the Liberals in the media might say, but don't, "a group of progressives") they are allowed to go on in peace and quiet planning for 1984. The fact that there is heavy Rockefeller (Chase Manhattan Bank and C.F.R.) influence in the media might also have something to do with the fact that while everybody has heard of, say, The John Birch Society (and almost always in a derogatory manner from the Eastern Establishment media), practically nobody has heard of the Bilderbergers.

As this is written, there have been 29 Bilderberger meetings to date. They usually last three days and are held in remote, but plush quarters. The participants are housed in one location and are protected by a thorough security network. Decisions are reached, resolutions adopted, plans of action initiated, but only Bilderbergers ever know for sure what occurred. We

106

Prince Bernhard of the Netherlands, head of the secret, one world Bilderberger movement, confers with President Nixon. A former Nazi SS storm trooper ("We had a lot of fun"), Bernhard now works with the Rothschilds and Communists to promote a World Super State of the elite.⑩ Bernhard holds yearly secret meetings with high U. S. officials, bankers and industrialists to map plans for merging the U. S. and the Soviet Union into a world government. After last meeting, Nixon devalued the dollar and opened up trade with Red China.

Edmond and Guy de Rothschild, leaders of the French Rothschild clan. The Rothschilds are closely connected with Prince Bernhard in business (Royal Dutch Shell) and in the building of a one world super-government with the Soviets. **Time** of Dec. 20, 1963, says of Guy: "Guy is every inch a Rothschild. He personifies much of what the family name stands for . . . He is a friend and confidante of some of France's politicians. . . . Most of all, he is dedicated to enlarging the fortune of his bank. . . . Guy heads a versatile clan of modern day Rothschilds." Edmond, reputedly the richest of the French Rothschilds, is worth $500 million personally, according to estimates.

must assume that these people did not congregate merely to discuss their golf scores. The press, naturally, is not allowed to be present, although occasionally a brief press conference is held at the end of the meeting at which time the news media are given in very general terms the Bilderberger version of what was discussed. Why all the secrecy if there is really nothing to hide? Why do the Ford, Rockefeller and Carnegie foundations finance the meetings if they are not important? Yes, why?

The most recent meeting took place at Laurance Rockefeller's Woodstock Inn at Woodstock, Vermont, April 23, 24, 25, 1971. Apparently the only newspaper to carry a substantial story on the meeting was the Rutland, Vermont, *Herald*, whose reporter could acquire only sketchy information about what the meeting was all about. The April 20, 1971 issue of the *Herald* reported:

> "A rather tight lid of secrecy was being kept on the conference. . . . A closed-door meeting was held in Woodstock last week to brief a handful of local officials on some phases of the conference. One participant of the meeting insisted Monday that the officials were told the meeting would be an 'international peace conference.' However, other reliable sources said the conference will deal with international finance. . . .
>
> The Woodstock Inn will apparently be sealed up like Fort Knox. . . . No press coverage will be allowed, with the exception of issuing a statement at the close of the meeting on Sunday."

When Prince Bernhard arrived at Boston's Logan Airport, he did admit to reporters that the subject of the conference would be the "change in the world-role of the United States." Isn't it nice to have changes in America's role in the world decided upon by Bernhard, Rothschild and Rockefeller? There is real democracy in action, as they say. Present at the scene to carry back orders to Mr. Nixon was C.F.R.-Rockefeller errand boy, the President's Number One advisor on foreign affairs, Henry Kissinger. Shortly after the Woodstock meeting, two ominous and "role changing" events occurred: Henry Kissinger went to Peking and arranged for the acceptance of Red China as a member of the family of trading nations; and an international monetary crisis developed after which the dollar was devalued. As the British statesman and Rothschild confidante Benjamin Disraeli wrote in *Coningsby:* "So you see, my dear Coningsby, that the world is governed by very different personages from what is imagined by those who are not behind the scenes."

(*Boston Committee)
(**Richard Nixon now claims that he no longer belongs to the C.F.R., having dropped out when the organization became an issue in his primary campaign for the governorship of California in 1962. Nixon has never said why he dropped out, but the fact that he has appointed over 110 C.F.R. members to important positions in his administration speaks for itself. It should come as no surprise that the very same Richard Nixon who campaigned in 1968 as a conservative had already made his real position very clear to the *Insiders* of the C.F.R. by authoring an article in the C.F.R. magazine, *Foreign affairs*, in October 1967. The title of this article, "Asia after Vietnam," revealed how the aspiring President Nixon would open a new policy toward Red China and bring "realism" to our Asian foreign policy.
    The C.F.R.'s Annual Report for 1952, admitted that sometimes members in sensitive positions were forced to go underground and keep the membership secret.)

Chapter VI

The Rockefellers and the Reds

The most important American of those "different personages" who run the world from behind the scenes are the Rockefellers. The Rockefeller clan reportedly has worked with the Rothschilds and their agents since the 1880's when the original John D. arranged to get a rebate on every barrel of oil he and his competitors shipped over Kuhn, Loeb & Co.-controlled Pennsylvania and Baltimore & Ohio railroads. It has been a profitable partnership ever since, although there appear to have been areas in which the two financial dynasties competed.

The involvement of the Rockefellers with their supposed blood enemies, the Communists, dates back to the Bolshevik Revolution. During the 1920's Lenin established his New Economic Policy (the same name Mr. Nixon applied to his wage-price control package), when the supposedly hated capitalists were invited back into Russia.

The Federal Reserve-CFR *Insiders* began pushing to open up Russia to U.S. traders soon after the revolution. However, at that time public opinion ran so high against the Bolsheviks because of their barbarism that it was official U. S. government policy not to deal with the outlaw government. The U. S. did not officially recognize the Bolsheviks until 1933. In the meantime, the Soviet economy was in a shambles and the people were starving to death. Communism would have collapsed had it not been aided by the *Insiders*. The Bolsheviks were originally saved from collapse by Herbert Hoover (CFR) who raised money to buy food which was appropriated by Lenin and his gangsters. They used it as a tool to subdue starving peasants who had been resisting their newly imposed slave masters. While Hoover's "humanitarian" gesture saved the Soviet regime, the Russian economy was still in total chaos. In came the Vanderlips, Harrimans and Rockefellers. One of the first to jump in was Frank Vanderlip, an agent of the Rockefellers and one of the Jekyl Island conspirators, president of the Rockefeller First National City Bank, who compared Lenin to George Washington.[1]

The Rockefellers assigned their public relations agent Ivy Lee, to sell the American public the idea that the Bolsheviks were merely misunderstood idealists who were actually kind benefactors of mankind.

Professor Antony Sutton of Stanford University's Hoover Institution, notes in his highly authoritative *Western Technology and Soviet Economic Development:*

> "Quite predictably, 180 pages later, Lee concludes that the communist problem is merely psychological. By this time he is talking about 'Russians' (not Communists) and concludes 'they are all right.' He suggests the United States should not engage in propaganda; makes a plea for peaceful coexistence; and suggests the United States would find it sound policy to recognize the USSR and advance credits."[2]

After the Bolshevik Revolution, Standard of New Jersey bought 50 percent of the Nobel's huge Caucasus oil fields even though the property had theoretically been nationalized.③

In 1927, Standard Oil of New York built a refinery in Russia, thereby helping the Bolsheviks put their economy back on its feet. Professor Sutton states: "This was the first United States investment in Russia since the Revolution."④

Shortly thereafter Standard Oil of New York and its subsidiary, Vacuum Oil Company, concluded a deal to market Soviet oil in European countries and it was reported that a loan of $75,000,000 to the Bolsheviks was arranged.⑤

We have been unable to find out if Standard Oil was even theoretically expropriated by the Communists. Sutton writes:

> "Only the Danish telegraph concessions, the Japanese fishing, coal and oil concessions, and the Standard Oil lease remained after 1935."⑥

Wherever Standard Oil would go, Chase National Bank was sure to follow. (The Rockefeller's Chase Bank was later merged with the Warburg's Manhattan Bank to form the present Chase Manhattan Bank.) In order to rescue the Bolsheviks, who were supposedly an archenemy, the Chase National Bank was instrumental in establishing the American-Russian Chamber of Commerce in 1922. President of the Chamber was Reeve Schley, a vice-president of Chase National Bank.⑦ According to Professor Sutton: "In 1925, negotiations between Chase and Prombank extended beyond the finance of raw materials and mapped out a complete program for financing Soviet raw material exports to the U. S. and imports of U. S. cotton and machinery.[8] Sutton also reports that "Chase National Bank and Equitable Trust Company were leaders in the Soviet credit business."[9]

The Rockefeller's Chase National Bank also was involved in selling Bolshevik bonds in the United States in 1928. Patriotic organizations denounced the Chase as an "international fence." Chase was called "a disgrace to America. . . . They will go to any lengths for a few dollars profits."[10] Congressman Louis McFadden, chairman of the House Banking Committee, maintained in a speech to his fellow Congressmen:

> "The Soviet government has been given United States Treasury funds by the Federal Reserve Board and the Federal Reserve Banks acting through the Chase Bank and the Guaranty Trust Company and other banks in New York City. . . .
>
> . . . Open up the books of Amtorg, the trading organization of the Soviet government in New York, and of Gostorg, the general office of the Soviet Trade Organization, and of the State Bank of the Union of Soviet Socialist Republics and you will be staggered to see how much American money has been taken from the United States' Treasury for the benefit of Russia. Find out what business has been transacted for the State Bank of Soviet Russia by its correspondent, the Chase Bank of New York; . . ."[11]

But the Rockefellers apparently were not alone in financing the Communist arm of the *Insiders'* conspiracy. According to Professor Sutton ". . . there is a report in the State Department files that names Kuhn, Loeb & Co. (the long-established and important financial house in New York) as the financier of the First Five Year Plan.⑫

Professor Sutton proves conclusively in his three volume history of Soviet technological development that the Soviet Union was almost literally manufactured by the U.S.A. Sutton quotes a report by Averell Harriman to the State Department in June, 1944 as stating:

"Stalin paid tribute to the assistance rendered by the United States to Soviet industry before and during the war. He said that about two-thirds of all the large industrial enterprise in the Soviet Union had been built with United States help or technical assistance."⑬

Remember that this was at a time when the Soviets had already established an extensive spy network in the U. S. and the Communist *Daily Worker* newspaper regularly called for the destruction of our liberty and the Sovietizing of America.

Sutton shows that there is hardly a segment of the Soviet economy which is not a result of the transference of Western, particularly American, technology.

This cannot be wholly the result of accident. For fifty years the Federal Reserve-CFR-Rockefeller-*Insider* crowd has advocated and carried out policies aimed at increasing the power of their satellite, the Soviet Union. Meanwhile, America spends $75 billion a year on defense to protect itself from the enemy the *Insiders* are building up.

What has been true of the past is even more valid today. The leader in promoting the transfer of technology and increasing aid and trade with the Communists is the Council on Foreign Relations.

On October 7, 1966, President Lyndon Johnson, a man who appointed a C.F.R. member to virtually every strategic position in his administration, stated:

"We intend to press for legislative authority to negotiate trade agreements which could extend most-favored-nation tariff treatment to European Communist states. . . .

We will reduce export controls on East-West trade with respect to hundreds of non-strategic items. . . ."

The *New York Times* reported one week later on—October 13, 1966:

"The United States put into effect today one of President Johnson's proposals for stimulating East-West trade by removing restrictions on the export of more than four hundred commodities to the Soviet Union and Eastern Europe. . . .

Among the categories from which items have been selected for export relaxation are vegetables, cereals, fodder, hides, crude and manufactured rubber, pulp and waste paper, textiles and textile fibers, crude fertilizers, metal ores and scrap, petroleum, gas and derivatives, chemical compounds and products, dyes, medicines, fireworks, detergents, plastic materials, metal products and machinery, and scientific and professional instruments."

Virtually every one of these "non-strategic" items has a direct or indirect use in war. Later, items such as rifle cleaning compounds, electronic equipment and radar were declared "non-strategic" and cleared for shipment to the Soviet Union. The trick simply is to declare almost everything "non-strategic." A machine gun is still considered strategic and therefore may not be shipped to the Communists, but the tools for making the machine guns and the chemicals to propel the bullets have been declared "non-strategic." Meanwhile, nearly 50,000 Americans have died in Vietnam. The Viet Cong and North Vietnamese receive 85 percent of their war materials from Russia and the Soviet bloc nations. Since their economies are incapable of supporting a war, the Communist arm of the conspiracy needed help from the Finance Capitalist arm. The United States has been financing and equipping both sides of the terrible Vietnamese war, killing our own soldiers by proxy. Again, the landscape painters in the mass media have kept the American public from learning this provable fact.

Not surprisingly, the Rockefellers have been leaders in championing this bloody trade. On January 16, 1967, one of the most incredible articles ever to appear in a newpaper graced the front page of the Establishment's daily, the *New York Times*. Under the headline "Eaton Joins Rockefellers To Spur Trade With Reds" the article stated:

> "An alliance of family fortunes linking Wall Street and the Midwest is going to try to build economic bridges between the free world and Communist Europe.
> The International Basic Economy Corporation, controlled by the Rockefeller brothers, and Tower International, Inc., headed by Cyrus S. Eaton Jr., Cleveland financier, plan to cooperate in promoting trade between the Iron Curtain countries, including the Soviet Union. . . ."

International Basic Economy Corporation (IBEC) is run by Richard Aldrich, grandson of Federal Reserve plotter Nelson Aldrich, and Rodman Rockefeller (CFR), Rocky's son. On October 20, 1969, IBEC announced that N. M. Rothschild & Sons of London had entered into partnership with the firm.

Cyrus Eaton Jr. is the son of the notoriously pro-Soviet Cyrus Eaton who began his career as secretary to John D. Rockefeller. It is believed that Eaton's rise to power in finance resulted from backing by his mentor. The agreement between Tower International and IBEC continues an old alliance. Al-

117

Nelson Rockefeller greets Khrushchev, the infamous "Butcher of Budapest." The Rockefeller and Eaton families have now joined forces to build war production plants behind the Iron Curtain so that the Communists can become a bigger threat to U. S. survival. America spends $70 billion a year ostensibly on defense and then the Rockefellers build aluminum mills for the Communists. Only the absence of a formal declaration of war in Vietnam keeps the Eatons and Rockefellers from being actionable for treason. They have the blood of nearly 50,000 American servicemen on their hands.

When Communist dictators visit the U. S. they do not visit laborers or union leaders, but hob-nob with industrial leaders. There is little, if any, attempt by the Red Dictators to identify with the working class. Here Nikita Khrushchev greets the avowedly pro-Communist industrialist Cyrus Eaton. Eaton started his business career as secretary to John D. Rockefeller and the Rockefeller family is believed to be largely responsible for his fortune.

though Eaton's name does not appear on the CFR's membership rolls, the Reece Committee which investigated foundations for Congress in 1953, found that Eaton was a secret member.

Among the "non-strategic" items which the Rockefeller-Eaton axis is going to build for the Communists are ten rubber goods plants, including two synthetic rubber plants worth $200 million. Mr. Eaton explains in the *Times* article: "These people are setting up new automobile plants and know they have to have tire factories." Under the Nixon Administration which, contrary to campaign promises, has multiplied trade with the Reds tenfold, American concerns are building the world's largest truck factory for the Communists. Trucks are necessary for a nation's war machine and truck factories can be converted to the production of tanks as was done during WWII. The U. S. will provide the Soviets with both the facilities to build the trucks and the tires (or tank treads) for them to roll on.

In addition, the Rockefellers and Eatons are constructing a $50 million aluminum producing plant for the Reds. Aluminum for jet planes is considered "non-strategic" under Johnson-Nixon doctrine.

Even more incredibly, the *Times* reveals:

> "Last month, Tower International reached a tentative agreement with the Soviet patent and licensing organization, Licensintorg, covering future licensing and patent transactions. Until now, Mr. Eaton said, the Russians have left the buying and selling of licenses and patents to the Amtorg Trading Corporation, the official Soviet agency in this country for promoting Soviet-American trade."

This means that the Rockefellers and Eatons have a monopoly on the transfer of technological capability to the supposed enemies of the super-rich, the Soviet Union. According to the *Times:*

"Mr. Eaton acknowledged the difficulties that Amtorg's representatives had encountered here in trying to arrange licensing agreements with American companies. 'As you can imagine,' he said, 'it is almost impossible for a Russian to walk into the research department of an American aerospace company and try to arrange the purchase of a patent'."

Certainly every loyal American will say to himself, "Well, I would hope to God the Soviets couldn't walk into our defense plants and buy a patent." The Rockefellers and the Eatons have solved that problem for the Communists. Now, instead of dealing with an official agency of the Soviet government, American concerns will be dealing with the Rockefellers. Meanwhile, nearly 50,000 Americans have died in Vietnam, many of them killed by weapons which the Rockefellers directly or indirectly supplied to our avowed enemies. Only the technicality of the lack of a formal declaration of war prevents the Rockefellers' trading in the blood of dead Americans from being actionable as treason.

Thus by the purchase of patents for the Communists the Rockefellers are virtually in charge of research and development for the Soviet military machine, allowing the Soviets to mass produce American developments. The transfer of such knowledge is even more important than the sale of weapons. A process that may have taken an American corporation a decade to develop is transferred *in toto* to the Communists. Does it make sense to spend $75 billion a year on national defense and then deliberately increase the war-making potential of an avowed enemy? It does to Mr. Rockefeller and the *Insiders*.

Since the Rockefellers have contracted to arrange for patents for the Soviets, they are by dictionary definition Communist agents. Would it not be more accurate to define the Communists as Rockefeller agents?

Indicative of this was a strange event which occurred in October of 1964. David Rockefeller, president of the Chase Manhattan Bank and chairman of the board of the Council on Foreign Relations, took a vacation in the Soviet Union. This is a peculiar place for the world's greatest "imperialist" to take his vacation since much of Communist propaganda deals with taking all of David's wealth away from him and distributing it to "the people." A few days after Rockefeller ended his "vacation" in the Kremlin, Nikita Khrushchev was recalled from a vacation at a Black Sea resort to learn that he had been fired. How strange! As far as the world knew, Khrushchev was the absolute dictator of the Soviet government and, more important, head of the Communist Party which runs the USSR. Who has the power to fire the man who was supposedly the absolute dictator? Did David Rockefeller journey to the Soviet Union to fire an employee? Obviously the position of premier in the Soviet Union is a figurehead with the true power residing elsewhere. Perhaps in New York.

For five decades the Communists have based their propaganda on the theme that they were going to destroy the Rockefellers and the other super-rich. Yet we find that for five decades the Rockefellers have been involved in building the strength of the Soviets. We are supposed to believe those international cartelists do this because they are foolish or greedy. Does this make sense? If a criminal goes up and down the streets shouting at the top of his lungs that as soon as he gets hold of a gun he is going to kill Joe Doaks, and you learn that Doaks is secretly giving guns to the criminal, one of two things must be true. Either Doaks is a fool or all the shouting is just "show biz" and the criminal secretly works for Doaks. The Rockefellers are not fools.

While David runs the financial end of the Rockefeller dynasty, Nelson runs the political. Nelson would like to be President of the United States. But, unfortunately for him, he is unacceptable to the vast majority of the grass roots of his own party. The next best thing to being President is con-

121

trolling a President. Nelson Rockefeller and Richard Nixon are supposed to be bitter political competitors. In a sense they are, but that still does not preclude Rockefeller from asserting dominion over Mr. Nixon. When Mr. Nixon and Mr. Rockefeller competed for the Republican nomination in 1968, Rockefeller naturally would have preferred to win the prize, but regardless of who won, he would control the highest office in the land.

You will recall that right in the middle of drawing up the Republican platform in 1960, Mr. Nixon suddenly left Chicago and flew to New York to meet with Nelson Rockefeller in what Barry Goldwater described as the "Munich of the Republican Party." There was no political reason why Mr. Nixon needed to crawl to Mr. Rockefeller. He had the convention all sewed up. The *Chicago* Tribune cracked that it was like Grant surrendering to Lee.

In *The Making of the President, 1960,* Theodore White noted that Nixon accepted all the Rockefeller terms for this meeting, including provisions "that Nixon telephone Rockefeller personally with his request for a meeting; that they meet at the Rockefeller apartment . . . that their meeting be secret and later announced in a press release from the Governor, not Nixon; that the meeting be clearly announced as taking place at the Vice President's request; that the statement of policy issuing from it be long, detailed, inclusive, not a summary communiqué."

The meeting produced the infamous "Compact of Fifth Avenue" in which the Republican Platform was scrapped and replaced by Rockefeller's socialist plans. The *Wall Street Journal* of July 25, 1960, commented: ". . . a little band of conservatives within the party . . . are shoved to the sidelines. . . . [T]he fourteen points are very liberal indeed; they comprise a platform akin in many ways to the Democratic platform and they are a far cry from the things that conservative men think the Republican Party ought to stand for. . . ." As Theodore White put it:

"Never had the quadrennial liberal swoop of the regulars been more nakedly dramatized than by the open compact of Fifth Avenue. Whatever honor they might have been able to carry from their services on the platform committee had been wiped out. A single night's meeting of the two men in a millionaire's triplex apartment in Babylon-by-the-Hudson, eight hundred and thirty miles away, was about to overrule them; they were exposed as clowns for all the world to see."

The whole story behind what happened in Rockefeller's apartment will doubtless never be known. We can only make an educated guess in light of subsequent events. But it is obvious that since that time Mr. Nixon has been in the Rockefeller orbit.

After losing to Kennedy by an eyelash, Mr. Nixon, against his wishes, and at the request (or order) of Rockefeller, entered the California gubernatorial race and lost. (For further details see the author's *Richard Nixon: The Man Behind the Mask*.) After losing to Pat Brown in the California gubernatorial race in 1962, Nixon had universally been consigned to the political trash heap. He left his practice as an attorney in California and went to New York, where he moved in as a neighbor of Nelson Rockefeller, the man who is supposedly his archenemy, in a $100,000-a-year apartment in a building owned by Rockefeller. Then Mr. Nixon went to work for the law firm of Mr. Rockefeller's personal attorney, John Mitchell, and in the next six years spent most of his time touring the country and the world, first rebuilding his political reputation and then campaigning to get the 1968 Republican nomination. At the same time, according to his own financial statement, his net worth multiplied many times and he became quite wealthy. Nelson Rockefeller, (and his colleagues of the Eastern Establishment), who helped make Nixon acceptable to Conservatives by appearing to oppose him, rescued Nixon from political oblivion and made him President of the United States. Does it not make sense that Mr. Nixon, the man of passionate ambition whose career had sunk to the bottom, had to make some deals in order to reach his goal? And did he not acquire massive political debts in return for being made President by the Eastern Liberal Establishment?

When Nixon left Washington, he, by his own claim, had little more than an old Oldsmobile automobile, Pat's respectable Republican cloth coat, and a government pension. While in law practice Nixon had an income of $200,000 per year, of which more than half went to pay for the apartment in Rocky's building. By 1968, he reported his net worth as $515,830, while assigning a value of only $45,000 to his partnership in his increasingly flourishing law firm. It may be that the frugal Mr. Nixon acquired the after-tax investment capital that mushroomed into $858,190 in assets by faithfully plugging his change into a piggy bank. Then again, it may have been part of Nixon's deal with Rockefeller and the *Insiders* that Mr. Nixon's personal poverty problems should be solved. The President is obviously an un-free agent.

The man most observers agree is the most powerful man in the Administration on domestic policy matters is Attorney General John Mitchell. Mitchell, who had been a Nixon law partner, served as campaign manager in 1968, and reportedly will serve in that capacity in 1972. The *Wall Street Journal* of January 17, 1969, revealed that Mitchell was Rocky's personal lawyer. The Establishment's landscape painters have etched a picture of Mitchell as a tough cop-type conservative bent; it appears that in reality Mitchell is but another Rockefeller agent.

Richard Nixon was elected President on a platform which promised to stop America's retreat before world Communism. Yet he appointed Henry Kissinger, a man who represented the opposite of the stands Mr. Nixon took during his campaign, to a position which is virtually Assistant President. Is it surprising then that Mr. Nixon has done just the opposite of what he promised he would do during his 1968 campaign?

How did Mr. Nixon come to pick an ultra-liberal to be his number one foreign policy advisor? We are told by *Time* magazine that Mr. Nixon met Kissinger at a cocktail party given by Clare Boothe Luce during the Christmas holidays in 1967. Mr. Nixon is supposed to have been so impressed by Dr. Kissinger's cocktail party repartee that he appointed him to the most powerful position in the Nixon Administration. Mr. Nixon would have to be stupid to have done that; and Mr. Nixon is not stupid. The Kissinger appointment was arranged by Nelson Rockefeller. (Salt Lack City *Desert News*, March 27, 1970.) Kissinger had served for five years as Rockefeller's personal advisor on foreign affairs and at the time of his appointment he was serving as a paid staff member of the Council on Foreign Relations.

Mr. Nixon's fantastic about face was praised by LBJ in the *Washington Star* of Dec. 1, 1971. The paper states:

"Former President Lyndon B. Johnson acknowledges that Richard Nixon, as a Republican President, has been able to accomplish some things that a Democratic President could not have. . . .

" 'Can't you just see the uproar,' he asked during a recent interview, 'if I had been responsible for Taiwan getting kicked out of the United Nations? Or if I had imposed sweeping national controls on prices and wages?'

" 'Nixon has gotten by with it,' he observed, an appreciative tone in his voice. 'If I had tried to do it, or Truman, or Humphrey, or any Democrat, we would have been clobbered.' "

Nelson Rockefeller and Richard Nixon are theoretically political enemies, but Rocky arranged '68 election so that if he could not be President, someone whom he controlled would be. The Rockefeller family, through their Chase Manhattan Bank and other entities, have been great benefactors of the Soviet Union ever since Communist Revolution in Russia. During campaign Nixon promised to halt shipment of war materials from America to North Vietnam via European Communist bloc because these supplies were being used to kill American soldiers. But much of this bloc trade is controlled by Rockefellers and Nixon has reversed himself and greatly multiplied such trade. The press, quite naturally, remains silent about killing American soldiers by proxy.

The boss and his two employees—the three musketeers of the CFR—Rocky, President Nixon and Henry Kissinger confer. Kissinger of Harvard was made virtual Assistant President by Rockefeller on whose staff he had served for a dozen years. Kissinger also had been on the staff of the CFR just prior to joining the Nixon Administration. Kissinger was the very embodiment of everything Nixon denounced during his '68 campaign. This explains why Nixon has reversed himself on so many stands. Among those to hail Mr. Nixon's move to the left is Alger Hiss, the Communist spy Richard Nixon helped convict. (**Chicago Tribune**, Oct. 25, 1971.) It was the Hiss Case which catapulted Nixon from obscurity into the Senate, the Vice Presidency and, eventually, the White House.

Chapter VII

Pressure from Above and
Pressure from Below

*T*HE ESTABLISHMENT'S official landscape artists have
done a marvelous job of painting a picture of Richard Nixon
as a conservative. Unfortunately, this picture is twenty years
out of date. The very liberal Senator Hugh Scott of Pennsylvania boasted to a reporter one day: "[Liberals] get the action
and the Conservatives get the rhetoric."① Richard Nixon could
not have been elected had he run as a Rockefeller liberal, but
he can get away with running his Administration like one
simply because the landscape painters fail to call the public's
attention to the fact. However, columnist Stewart Alsop in
writing for a sophisticated audience of approving Liberals,
reveals the real Nixon. Alsop claims that if Nixon were judged
by his deeds instead of his ancient image, the Liberals' attitude
toward him would be different. If only the Liberals' Pavlovian
response to the Nixon name could be eliminated, says Alsop,
they would realize how far Left he is. Therefore Alsop substi-
tutes a hypothetical "President Liberal" for President Nixon:

". . . If President Liberal were actually in the
White House, it is not at all hard to imagine the re-

action to his program. The right would be assailing President Liberal for bugging out of Vietnam, undermining American defenses, fiscal irresponsibility, and galloping socialism. The four basic Presidential policy positions listed above would be greeted with hosannas by the liberals. . . .

Instead, the liberals have showered the President with dead cats, while most conservatives have maintained a glum silence, and thus the Administration has been 'little credited' for 'much genuine achievement.' But there are certain special reasons, which Pat Moynihan omitted to mention, why this is so."②

Alsop further explains how having the reputation of being an enemy of the Liberal Democrats helps Nixon pass their program:

"For one thing, there is a sort of unconscious conspiracy between the President and his natural enemies, the liberal Democrats, to conceal the extent to which his basic program, leaving aside frills and rhetoric, is really the liberal Democratic program. Richard Nixon is the first professional politician and 'real Republican' to be elected President in 40 years—and it is not in the self-interest of the liberals to give credit to such a President for liberal initiatives. By the same token, it is not in the self-interest of the President to risk his conservative constituency by encouraging the notion that he is not a 'real Republican' after all, but a liberal Democrat at cut rates. . . .

There are plenty of examples of the mutual obfuscation which results from this mutual interest. The withdrawal of half a million men from Vietnam is quite obviously the greatest retreat in American history. But the President talks as though it were somehow a glorious advance, certain to guarantee a 'just and lasting peace.' When the President—like any commander of a retreat—resorts to spoiling actions to protect his dwindling rear guard, the liberals howl that he is 'chasing the will-o'-the-wisp of military victory.'

. . . When the President cuts back real military strength more sharply than in a quarter of a century, the liberals attack him for failing to 'reorder priorities.' The President, in his rhetoric about a 'strong defense,' plays the same game. The result, as John Kenneth Galbraith accurately noted recently, is that 'most people and maybe most congressmen think the Administration is indulging the Pentagon even more than the Democrats,' which is the precise opposite of the truth. . . ."

Alsop continued what is probably the most damning column ever written about Richard Nixon by noting the role that the mass media have played in portraying to the public an image that is the reverse of the truth:

". . . There is also a human element in this exercise in mutual obfuscation. To the liberals, especially the liberal commentators who dominate the media, Richard Nixon is Dr. Fell ('The reason why I cannot tell, but this I know and know full well, I do not like thee, Dr. Fell.'). This is not surprising. Not too many years ago, Richard M. Nixon was one of the most effective—and least lovable—of the conservative Republican professionals of the McCarthy era."

The columnist, himself a member of the socialist Americans for Democratic Action (ADA), speculated on what the "old Nixon" would have had to say about the "new Nixon":

". . . on his past record, it is not at all hard to imagine R. M. Nixon leading the assault on the President for his 'bug-out,' 'fiscal irresponsibility,' 'galloping socialism,' and all the rest of it. So how can one expect Mr. Nixon to defend President Liberal's program with the passionate conviction that a President Robert Kennedy, say, would have brought to the defense of such a program?"[3]

Alsop has revealed the *real* Nixon and is obviously pleased. Those who voted for Nixon shouldn't be quite so happy. If you liked the Richard Nixon who ran for the Presidency, then you cannot, if you are consistent, like the Richard Nixon who is President. Nixon and his fellow "moderates" have turned the Republican elephant into a donkey in elephant's clothing. On June 19, 1959, Vice President Nixon gloated: "In summary, the Republican administration produced the things that the Democrats promised." It looks as if it's haping again!

A year and a half earlier Nixon had been warbling a different tune:

> "If we have nothing to offer other than a pale carbon copy of the New Deal, if our only purpose is to gain and retain power, the Republican Party no longer has any reason to exist, and ought to go out of business."[4]

The Nixon "Game Plan," as Harvard Professor John Kenneth Galbraith gleefully points out, is SOCIALISM. The Nixon "Game Plan" is infinitely more clever and dangerous than those of his predecessors because it masquerades as being the opposite of what it is.

Mr. Nixon is aware that most Americans fear "big government." An August 1968, Gallup Poll showed that 46 percent of the American public believed that "big government" was the "biggest threat to the country." Gallup commented:

"Although big government has been a favorite Republican target for many years, rank and file democrats are nearly as critical of growing Federal power as are Republicans."⑨ Recognizing this attitude, Mr. Nixon geared much of his campaign rhetoric to attacking Big Daddy government. However, the Nixon Administration has taken massive steps to further concentrate authority in the federal "power pinnacle." (See Chart 3, p. 33.)

While centralizing power at a rate which would have made Hubert Humphrey blush, Mr. Nixon has continued to pay lip service to decentralization. During the first year of his Administration Mr. Nixon announced his "New Federalism" (the name taken from the title of a book by Nelson Rockefeller). The first part of the "New Federalism" is the Family Assistance Program (FAP) which would, contrary to his campaign promises, provide a Guaranteed Annual Income. Based on suggestions from John Gardner of the C.F.R. and Daniel Moynihan, a member of the board of directors of the socialist ADA, the FAP would double the number on welfare and increase tremendously the power of the executive branch of the federal government. The Leftwing weekly, the *New Republic*, cheered the proposal as "creeping socialism."

The second major segment of the President's "New Federalism" is revenue sharing with the states, touted as a step in the decentralization of power from the federal government. Actually, the program does just the opposite. The money must first go from the states to Washington before it can be shared. As columnist James J. Kilpatrick remarked: ". . . power to control follows the Federal dollar as surely as that famous lamb accompanied little Mary." As soon as the states and local governments get hooked on the federal funds, the controls will be put on just as they were in education and agriculture. Every field the government attempts to take over it first subsidizes. You can't decentralize government by centralizing the tax collections.

Mr. Nixon's "power to the people" slogan really means

"power to the President."

House Ways and Means Chairman Wilbur Mills has called the revenue-sharing plan a "trap" that "could become a massive weapon against the independence of state and local government." The plan, said Mills, "goes in the direction of centralized government."

But, Mr. Nixon is very clever. In his 1971 State of the Union Message, the talk in which he used the Communist slogan "Power to the People," the President said:

> "We in Washington will at last be able to provide government that is truly for the people. I realize that what I am asking is that not only the Executive branch in Washington, but that even this Congress will have to change by giving up some of its power."⑥

That sounds reasonable doesn't it? The Executive branch will give up some power and the Congress will give up some power and the people will gain by having these powers returned to them. Right? Wrong! That is nothing but verbal sleight of hand. Notice the precision of Mr. Nixon's language. He speaks of the "Executive branch *in Washington*" giving up some of its power. Three days later it became obvious why Mr. Nixon added the seemingly redundant "in Washington" when it was announced that the country was being carved up into ten federal districts. These federal districts would soon be used as the mysterious League of Just Men had hired Karl Marx to in the federal government almost total power over the economy.

To many political observers the most shocking development of the past year was the admission by President Richard Nixon to newsman Howard K. Smith that he is "now a Keynesian in economics." The jolted Smith commented later, "That's a little like a Christian Crusader saying: 'All things considered, I think Mohammed was right." Howard K. Smith was well aware that such a statement was tantamount to a declaration by Mr. Nixon that "I am now a Socialist." John Maynard Keynes, the English economist and Fabian Socialist, bragged that he was promoting the "euthanasia of capitalism."

It is generally believed in England among students of this conspiracy that John Maynard Keynes produced his *General Theory of Money and Credit* at the behest of certain *Insiders* of international finance who hired him to concoct a pseudo-scientific justification for government deficit spending—just as the mysterious League of Just Men had hired Karl Marx to write the *Communist Manifesto*. The farther a government goes into debt, the more interest is paid to the powerful *Insiders* who "create" money to buy government bonds by the simple expedient of bookkeeping entries. Otherwise, you can bet your last farthing that the *Insiders* of international banking would be violently opposed to inflationary deficits.

In his internationally syndicated column of February 3, 1971, James Reston (C.F.R.) exclaimed:

> "The Nixon budget is so complex, so unlike the Nixon of the past, so un-Republican that it defies rational analysis. . . . The Nixon budget is more planned, has more welfare in it, and has a bigger predicted deficit than any other budget in this century."

During 1967, while on the primary trail, Richard Nixon made exorbitant Democrat spending his Number Two campaign issue, just behind the failure of the Democrats to win the Vietnam War. Mr. Johnson's 1967 Budget was $158.6 billion, which at the time seemed astronomical. Mr. Nixon claimed that if that amount were not sliced by $10 billion the country faced financial disaster. At a time when the Vietnam War was a far bigger financial drain than it is now, Richard Nixon argued that we should be spending around $150 billion. President Nixon is now spending $230 billion, and bills already introduced in Congress and likely to pass could push the 1972 Fiscal Budget (July 1, 1971 to July 1, 1972) to $250 billion.

The point is that the man who campaigned as Mr. Frugal in 1968 is, in his third year of office, out-spending by $80 to $100 billion what he said his predecessor should spend. And some experts are predicting that Mr. Nixon could spend as much as $275 billion next year.

This is the same Richard Nixon who in Dallas on October 11, 1968, declared that "America cannot afford four years of Hubert Humphrey in the White House" because he had advocated programs which would have caused "a spending spree that would have bankrupted this nation." Candidate Nixon flayed the Johnson Administration for failing "to cut deficit spending which is the cause of our present inflation." Budget deficits, he said, "lie at the heart of our troubles." For his own part, he renounced any "massive step-up" in federal spending. "This is a prescription for further inflation," said Nixon. "I believe it is also a prescription for economic disaster."

While it took LBJ five years to run up a $55 billion deficit, Senator Harry Byrd notes that the accumulated deficit for Mr. Nixon's first *three* years will reach at least $88 billion. Congressional experts are now predicting Richard Nixon could well pour on the red ink to a total of $124 billion in this term of office alone.

In order to halt inflation Mr. Nixon has now instituted wage and price controls. Most Americans, sick of seeing their paychecks shrink in purchasing power each month, have overwhelmingly approved. But this is because most people are not aware of the real causes of inflation. And you can be sure that the Establishment's landscape painters will not explain the truth to them. The truth is that there is a difference between inflation and the wage-price spiral. When the government runs a deficit, brand new money in the amount of the deficit is put into circulation. As the new money percolates through the economy it bids up wages and prices. This is easy to under-

136

stand if you think of our economy as a giant auction. Just as at any other auction, if the bidders are suddenly supplied with more money, they will use that money to bid up prices. Inflation, in reality, is an increase in the supply of money. It causes the wage-price spiral which is generally mislabeled *inflation*. You could not have a wage price spiral if you did not have an increase in the money supply with which to pay it. This is not just economics, it is physics. You can't fill a quart bottle with a pink of milk. To say that the wage-spiral causes inflation is like saying wet streets cause rain. Mr. Nixon, unlike the vast majority of the American public, is aware of the real causes of "inflation." He explained it clearly on January 27, 1970:

> "The inflation we have at the start of the Seventies was caused by heavy deficit spending in the Sixties. In the past decade, the Federal Government spent more than it took in—$57 billion more. These deficits caused prices to rise 25 percent in a decade."

Business blames "inflation" on the unions, and unions blame "inflation" on business, but only the government can cause "inflation."

Mr. Nixon has fastened wage and price controls on the economy supposedly to solve a problem which Mr. Nixon (and LBJ) created by running huge deficits. If he sincerely wanted to stop "inflation" he would have put wage and price controls on the government rather than on the rest of us and would have stopped deficit spending. People are cheering Nixon because he "did something." This is akin to cheering for a motorist who shoots a pedestrian he has just run over.

Wage and price controls are at the very heart of Socialism. You can't have a totalitarian government without wage and price controls and you can't have a free country with them. Why? You cannot impose slavery upon people who have economic freedom. As long as people have economic freedom,

137

they will be free. Wage and price controls are people controls. In his Phase II speech, Mr. Nixon made it clear that the 90-day wage and price controls are with us in one disguise or another from now on. They are a major step towards establishing an all-powerful Executive branch of the federal government.

After the *Insiders* have established the United Socialist States of America (in fact if not in name), the next step is the Great Merger of all nations of the world into a dictatorial world government. This was the main reason behind the push to bring Red China into the United Nations. If you want to control the natural resources, transportation, commerce and banking for the whole world, you must put everybody under the same roof.

The *Insiders'* code word for the world superstate is "new world order," a phrase often used by Richard Nixon. The Council on Foreign Relations states in its *Study No. 7:* "The U. S. must strive to: A. BUILD A NEW INTERNATIONAL ORDER." (Capitals in the original) Establishment spokesman James Reston (CFR) declared in his internationally syndicated column for the *New York Times* of May 21, 1971: "Nixon would obviously like to preside over the creation of a new world order, and believes he has an opportunity to do so in the last 20 months of his first term."

A world government has always been the object of the Communists. In 1915, in No. 40 of the Russian organ, *The Socialist Democrat,* Lenin proposed a "United States of the World." The program of the Communist International of 1936 says that world dictatorship "can be established only by victory of socialism in different countries or groups of countries, after which the Proletariat Republics would unite on federal lines with those already in existence, and this system would expand . . . at length forming the world union of Soviet Socialist Republics."

One of the most important groups promoting the "world union" is the United World Federalists, whose membership is heavily interlocked with that of the Council on Foreign Relations. The UWF advocate turning the UN into a full-fledged world government which would include the Communist nations.

Richard Nixon is, of course, far too clever to actually join the UWF, but he has supported their legislative program since his early days in Congress. In the October 1948 issue of the UWF publication *World Government News*, on page 14, there appears the following announcement: "Richard Nixon: Introduced world government resolution (HCR 68) 1947, and ABC (World Government) resolution 1948."

World government has a strong emotional appeal for Americans, based on their universal desire for world peace. The *Insiders* have the Communists rattling their sabers with one hand and dangling the olive branch with the other. Naturally everyone gravitates towards the olive branch, not realizing that the olive branch is controlled by another arm of the entity that is rattling the sabers.

In September of 1968, candidates for public office received a letter from the United World Federalists that stated:

"Our organization has been endorsed and commended by all U. S. presidents in the last 20 years and by the current nominees for the presidency. As examples we quote as follows:

Richard Nixon: 'Your organization can perform an important service by continuing to emphasize that world peace can only come thru world law. Our goal is world peace. Our instrument for achieving peace will be law and justice. If we concentrate our energies toward these ends, I am hopeful that real progress can be made.'

Hubert Humphrey: 'Every one of us is committed to brotherhood among all nations, but no one pursues these goals with more dignity and dedication than the United World Federalists.' "⑦

There really was not a dime's worth of difference. Voters were given the choice between CFR world government advocate Nixon and CFR world government advocate Humphrey. Only the rhetoric was changed to fool the public.

A world government requires a world supreme court, and Mr. Nixon is on record in favor of a world supreme court. And a world government must have a world police force to enforce the laws of the World Superstate and keep the slaves from rebelling. The *Los Angeles Examiner* of October 28, 1950, reported that Congressman Richard Nixon had introduced a "resolution calling for the establishment of a United Nations police force. . . ."

Not surprisingly, the *Insiders* have their pet planners preparing to administrate their world dictatorship. Under an immense geodetic dome at Southern Illinois University is a completely detailed map of the world which occupies the space of three football fields. Operating under grants from the Ford, Carnegie and Rockefeller foundations (all extensively interlocked with the C.F.R.) a battery of scientists including everything from geographers, psychologists and behavioral scientists to natural scientists, biologists, biochemists and agronomists are making plans to control people. These elite planners conduct exercises in what they call "the world game." For example: There are too many people in Country A and not enough people in Country B. How do you move people from Country A to Country B? We need so many males, so many females, so many of this occupation and so many of that occupation, so many of this age and so many of that age. How do you get these people from Country A and settle them in Country B in the shortest possible time? Another example: We have an uprising in Country C (or as it would now be called, District C) How long does it take to send in "peace" forces to stop the insurgency?

The World Game people run exercises on global control. If you plan on running the world, you cannot go about it haphazardly. That is why the *Insiders* of the Ford, Carnegie and Rockefeller foundations are making these plans. The real name of the game is *1984*. We will have systematic population reduction, forced sterilization or anything else which the planners deem necessary to establish absolute control in their *humanitarian* utopia. But to enforce these plans, you must have an all-powerful world government. You can't do this if individual nations have sovereignty. And before you can facilitate the Great Merger, you must first centralize control within each nation, destroy the local police and remove the guns from the hands of the citizenry. You must replace our once free Constitutional Republic with an all-powerful central government. And that is exactly what is happening today with the Nixon Administration. Every action of any consequence, despite the smokescreen, has centralized more power in what is rapidly becoming an all-powerful central government.

What we are witnessing is the Communist tactic of *pressure from above and pressure from below*, described by Communist historian Jan Kozak as the device used by the Reds to capture control of Czecho-Slovakia. The pressure from above comes from secret, ostensibly respectable Comrades in the government and Establishment, forming, with the radicalized mobs in the streets below, a giant pincer around middle-class society. The street rioters are pawns, shills, puppets, and dupes for an oligarchy of elitist conspirators working above to turn America's limited government into an unlimited government with total control over our lives and property.

The American middle-class is being squeezed to death by a vise. (See Chart 9) In the streets we have avowed revolutionary groups such as the Students for a Democratic Society (which was started by the League for Industrial Democracy, a group with strong C.F.R. ties), the Black Panthers, the Yippies, the Young Socialist Alliance. These groups chant that if we don't "change" America, we will lose it. "Change" is a word we hear over and over. By "change" these groups mean Socialism. Virtually all members of these groups sincerely believe that they are fighting the Establishment. In reality they are an in-

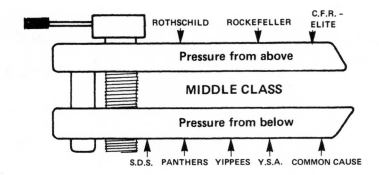

dispensible ally of the Establishment in fastening Socialism on all of us. The naive radicals think that under Socialism the "people" will run everything. Actually, it will be a clique of *Insiders* in total control, consolidating and controlling all wealth. That is why these schoolboy Lenins and teenage Trotskys are allowed to roam free and are practically never arrested or prosecuted. They are protected. If the Establishment wanted the revolutionaries stopped, how long do you think they would be tolerated?

Instead, we find that most of these radicals are the recipients of largesse from major foundations or are receiving money from the government through the War on Poverty. The Rothschild-Rockefeller-C.F.R. *Insiders* at the top "surrender to the demands" for Socialism from the mobs below. The radicals are doing the work of those whom they hate the most.

Remember Bakunin's charge that Marx' followers had one foot in the bank and the other in the Socialist movement.

Further indications of Establishment financing of the Communist S.D.S. are contained in James Kunen's *The Strawberry Statement: Notes of A College Revolutionary.* Describing events at the 1968 S.D.S. national convention, Kunen says:

142

"Also at the convention, men from Business International Roundtables—the meetings sponsored by Business International—tried to buy up a few radicals. These men are the world's leading industrialists and they convene to decide how our lives are going to go. These are the boys who wrote the Alliance for Progress. They're the left wing of the ruling class.

They agreed with us on black control and student control. . . .

They want McCarthy in. They see fascism as the threat, see it coming from Wallace. The only way McCarthy could win is if the crazies and young radicals act up and make Gene look more reasonable. They offered to finance our demonstrations in Chicago.

We were also offered Esso (Rockefeller) money. They want us to make a lot of radical commotion so they can look more in the center as they move to the left."[8]

THAT IS THE STRATEGY. THE LANDSCAPE PAINTERS FOCUS YOUR ATTENTION ON THE KIDS IN THE STREET WHILE THE REAL DANGER IS FROM ABOVE.

As Frank Capell recently observed in *The Review Of The News:*

"Of course, we know that these radical students are not going to take over the government. What they are going to do is provide the excuse for the government to take over the people, by passing more and more repressive laws to 'keep things under control.'"

The radicals make a commotion in the streets while the Limousine Liberals at the top in New York and Washington are Socializing us. WE ARE GOING TO HAVE A DICTA-TORSHIP OF THE ELITE DISGUISED AS A DICTA-TORSHIP OF THE PROLETARIAT.

Now the *Insiders* of the Establishment are moving into a more sophisticated method of applying pressure from below. John Gardner, a "Republican" and member of the C.F.R., has established a grass roots proletarian organization called Common Cause. This may become the biggest and most important organization in American history. Common Cause's goal is to organize welfare recipients, those who have not voted before, and Liberals to lobby for Socialism. That lobbying will not only be expressed in pressuring Congress to pass Socialist legislation but will also be expressed as ballot power in elections. Common Cause is supposedly the epitome of anti-Establishmentarianism, but who is paying the bills? The elite *Insider* radicals from above. The number one bankroller of this group to overthrow the super-rich and re-distribute their wealth among the poor is John D. Rockefeller III. Other key financiers are Andrew Heiskell (CFR), chairman of the board of Time, Inc., Thomas Watson (CFR), chairman of the board of IBM, John Whitney (CFR) of the Standard Oil fortune, Sol Linowitz (CFR), chairman of the board of Xerox, and Gardner Cowles (CFR) of Cowles publications. In any organization, the man who pays the bills is the boss. The others are his employees.⑨

What better proof could we have that Socialism is not a movement of downtrodden masses but of power hungry elitists? The poor are merely pawns in the game. Needless to say, the landscape painters hide Common Cause's financial angels so that only those who understand that the Establishment's game plan is SOCIALISM understand what is going on before their very eyes.

144

Chapter VIII

You Are the Answer

M_{ANY} people cannot refrain from rationalizing. After reading this book, some will bemoan the fact that the situation is hopeless. These will be many of the same people who, before reading this book, really did not believe the problems facing us were serious. Some people wake up and give up in the same week. This is, of course, just exactly what the *Insiders* want you to do.

The conspiracy *can* be defeated. The *Insiders* are not omnipotent. It is true that they control important parts of the federal government, high finance and the mass media. But they do not control everything, or the vise would already have been closed. We might say the conspiracy controls everything but you. *You* are their Achilles heel if you are willing to fight. There is an old cliche in sports that quitters never win and winners never quit. We need a million Americans who are *not* quitters, but, moreover, who have the will to win!

Of course, you can't buck the conspiracy head on. . . . trying to fight it on its home grounds. But the *Insiders* are vulnerable to an end run. You, and thousands of others like you can make an end run if you want to. It is our intention in this closing chapter to show why it can be done and how you can do it.

The timing for an end run has never been better. What Barry Goldwater said in 1964, people were willing to believe in 1968. Most people who voted for Nixon did so because he promised to balance the budget, not establish wage and price controls; slash government spending, not multiply it; cut welfare, not push for a guaranteed annual income; stand firm against the Communists, not lead the Red Chinese into the U.N.; build America's defenses, not continue to unilaterally disarm us; and stop aid and trade with our avowed Communist enemies, not double it. These were the issues which supposedly differentiated Nixon from Humphrey. Now we see that Nixon has repudiated his own promises and carried out those of his opponent. By 1972, millions of Americans will have concluded that there is little difference between the leadership of the two major parties. And more and more people are beginning to realize that there is a tiny clique of conspirators at the top which controls both the Democrat and Republican Parties.

The one thing these conspirators cannot survive is exposure. The *Insiders* are successful only because so few of their victims know what is being planned and how *Insiders* are carrying out those plans. Conspiracies can operate only in the dark. They cannot stand the truthful light of day. Once any sizeable minority of the American people becomes aware of the conspiracy and what it is up to, the many decades of patient planning and work by the *Insiders* in this country can be destroyed in an amazingly short period of time.

This job is largely a matter of getting others to realize that they have been conned and are continuing to be conned. You must become the local arm of the world's largest floating university. But before you can go to work, pointing out these conspiratorial facts to others, you must know the facts yourself. This book is designed to give you these facts, and can be your greatest tool. It is available on tape casettes* so that you can virtually memorize its contents by listening to it repeatedly while you are washing the dishes or driving to and from work. The concept of an army of individuals which is dedicated to exposing "the conspiracy" frightens the *Insiders* because it works outside the channels which they control.

Richard Nixon has said of the Republican Party: "We've got to have a tent everyone can get into." The Democrats have obviously believed that for a long time. But a Party must be based on principles or it has no justification for existence. Bringing Socialists into the Republican Party theoretically may broaden the base, but, in reality, serves only to disfranchise those who believe in a Constitutional Republic and the free enterprise system.

In 1972, the Republicans will try to make you forget that Richard Nixon was elected on George Wallace's platform but has been carrying out Hubert Humphrey's. The pitch will be "party unity." "If not Nixon then who?" will be the typical response to complaints about Nixon's actions. But unity with evil is evil. During the campaign of 1972, Nixon will again *talk* conservatively while the C.F.R.'s Democrat candidate will sound frighteningly radical in order to stampede you into accepting Nixon as the lesser of two evils. The Establishment may even run its John Lindsay or Eugene McCarthy as a far Left third or fourth party candidate in order to split the Democratic Party and re-elect Richard Nixon with a comparatively small number of votes.

It is only logical that the *Insiders* will try to apply the *coup de grace* against America through a Republican President simply because most people cannot believe that a Republican could be "soft on Communism" or would jeopardize our liberty or sovereignty. The watchdogs tend to go to sleep with a Republican in office.

Democrats and Republicans must break the *Insider* control of their respective parties. The C.F.R.-types and their flunkies and social climbing opportunist supporters must be invited to leave or else the Patriots must leave.

149

It is up to you to put the politicians on the spot and make the C.F.R.-*Insiders* a campaign issue. This can be accomplished easily by creating the base of thinking that will oppose their positions. The Socialists must be forced to gather into one party. The conspiracy doesn't want the resultant clear distinction between party ideologies. The *Insiders* want the issues between the parties to be cloudy and gray, centering on personalities, not principles. Neither party can come out strongly against Socialism as long as it is pushing Socialist programs. But that is the way the *Insiders* want it.

The issue, very simply, is the enslavement of you and your children. Just because many of these *Insiders* are theoretically Americans, don't think they will spare this country the terror they have brought to thirty others through their hired Communist thugs. To the *Insiders*, the world is their country and their only loyalty is to themselves and their fellow conspirators. Being an American means no more to them than being an honorary citizen of Bali would mean to you. It has not bothered their consciences one iota that millions of your fellow human beings have been murdered, including 50,000 of your own sons in Vietnam. In order to solidify their power in the United States they will need to do here the same thing they have done in other countries. They will establish and maintain their dictatorship through stark terror. The terror does not end with the complete takeover of the Republic. Rather, then terror just begins . . . for total, all encompassing terror is an absolute necessity to keep a dictatorship in power. And terror does not mean merely punishing the enemies of the New Order. Terror requires the murdering and imprisoning of people at random . . . even many of those who helped them come to power.

Those who are complacent and hope to escape the terror because they were not involved in politics or resisted the New Order coming to power must be made, by you, to understand that this all-encompassing need for terror includes *them* especially . . . that they cannot escape by doing nothing.

What can we expect from the conspiracy during the next few years? Here are fourteen signposts on the road to totalitarianism compiled some years ago by historian Dr. Warren Carrol and a refugee from Yugoslavian Communism, Mike Djordjevich. The list is not in any particular order nor is the order of any particular significance as given here. But the imposition of any one of these new restrictions on liberty (none of which was in effect when the list was compiled) would be a clear warning that the totalitarian state is very near; and once a significant number of them—perhaps five has been imposed, we can rationally conclude that the remainder would not be far behind and that the fight for freedom and the preservation of the Republic has been lost in this country.

FOURTEEN SIGNPOSTS TO SLAVERY

1. Restrictions on taking money out of the country and on the establishment or retention of a foreign bank account by an American citizen.

2. Abolition of private ownership of hand guns.

3. Detention of individuals without judicial process.

4. Requirements that private financial transactions be keyed to social security numbers or other government identification so that government records of these transactions can be kept and fed into a computer.

5. Use of compulsory education laws to forbid attendance at presently existing private schools.

6. Compulsory non-military service.

7. Compulsory psychological treatment for non-government workers or public school children.

8. An official declaration that anti-Communist organizations are subversive and subsequent legal action taken to suppress them.

9. Laws limiting the number of people allowed to meet in a private home.

10. Any significant change in passport regulations to make passports more difficult to obtain or use.

151

11. Wage and price controls, especially in a non-wartime situation.

12. Any kind of compulsory registration with the government of where individuals work.

13. Any attempt to restrict freedom of movement within the United States.

14. Any attempt to make a new major law by executive decree (that is, actually put into effect, not merely authorized as by existing executive orders.)

As you are no doubt aware President Nixon already has invoked numbers 1, 11 and 14.

Steps 2, 3, 6, 7, 9, 12 and 13 already have been proposed and some are actively campaigned for by organized groups. As of January 1, 1972, banks must report to the government any deposit or withdrawal over $5,000.① The next step will be to restrict the taking of money out of the country. Big Brother is watching your bank account!

Increased government control over many kinds of private schools is proposed annually in many state legislatures. Compulsory non-military service—a universal draft of all young men and women, with only a minority going into the armed services has been discussed by the Nixon Administration as an alternative to the draft. Sensitivity training is already required for an increasing number of government workers, teachers and school children. As long ago as 1961, Victor Reuther proposed that anti-Communist groups and organizations be investigated and placed on the Attorney General's subversive list. The propaganda war in progress to force registration or confiscation of firearms is the number one priority of all the collectivists—an armed citizenry is the major roadblock to a totalitarian takeover of the United States.

You are in this fight whether you want to be or not. Unless you are an *Insider*, you are a victim. Whether you are a multimillionaire or a pauper you have an enormous amount at stake.

The *Insiders* are counting on your being too preoccupied with your own problems or too lazy to fight back while the chains of slavery are being fastened on you. They are counting on their mass media to con you, frighten you, or ridicule you out of saving your freedom, and, most of all, they are counting on your thinking you can escape by not taking part in opposing their takeover.

They are also counting on those of you who recognize the conspiracy becoming so involved with watching all moves that you become totally mesmerized by their machinations, and thus become incapable of acting.

The choice is yours. You can say, "It can't happen here!" But nearly every one of the one billion people enslaved by the Communists since 1945 doubtless said the same thing. Or you can *end run* this whole conspiratorial apparatus.

The choice you must make was enunciated by Winston Churchill when he told the people of England:

> "If you will not fight for right when you can easily win without bloodshed; if you will not fight when your victory will be sure and not too costly; you may come to the moment when you will have to fight with all the odds against you and only a precarious chance of survival."

Because we have ignored warning after warning, we are now at that place in history. Unless you do your part now, you will face a further choice, also described by Mr. Churchill. He said:

> "There may be even a worse fate. You may have to fight when there is no hope of victory, because it is better to perish than live as slaves."

Appendix I

COUNCIL ON FOREIGN RELATIONS/TRILATERAL COMMISSION INFLUENCE IN THE REAGAN ADMINISTRATION

The Council on Foreign Relations, founded by a small group of internationalists in 1919, continues to be the largest *American* organization of Insiders working for a "New World Order." In 1973 a new *international* organization was formed by C.F.R. Chairman David Rockefeller, however. Consisting of key government officials and opinion molders in the United States, Europe, and Japan, the new group was called the Trilateral Commission.

> *The Council on Foreign Relations is the American branch of a society which originated in England... (and)... believes national boundaries should be obliterated and one-world rule established.*
>
> *The Trilateral Commission is international... (and)... is intended to be the vehicle for multi-national consolidation of the commercial and banking interests by seizing control of the political government of the United States.*
>
> Senator Barry Goldwater
> **With No Apologies**

Although as a *candidate* Ronald Reagan denounced the internationalist loyalities of the Council on Foreign Relations and the Trilateral Commission, as *President* he has appointed many of their members to key government positions. C.F.R./Trilateral Commission members control the Vice Presidency, State Department, Defense Department, Treasury Department, Central Intelligence Agency, the Commerce Department, and the Department of Labor.

A more detailed listing of "Insider" influence in the Reagan

155

Administration follows. It is important to note that, *even without a single C.F.R./T.C. member in the Reagan Administration,* "Insider" influence in Washington and throughout the country would still be immense. In the pages that follow, we have indicated just *some* of the major centers of influence controlled by members of this elitist cabal.

Key Reagan Appointees

George Bush, *Vice President*, CFR/TC
George Schultz, *Secretary of State*, CFR
Casper Weinberger, *Secretary of Defense*, CFR/TC
Gen. David Jones, *Chairman, Joint Chiefs of Staff*, CFR
William Casey, *Director, Central Intelligence Agency*, CFR
Donald Regan, *Secretary of the Treasury*, CFR
Robert Anderson, *Secretary of Labor*, CFR
Malcolm Baldrige, *Secretary of Commerce*, CFR

Other Reagan Appointees

H. B. Chenery, *World Bank*, CFR
W.B. Dale, *International Monetary Fund*, CFR
Henry Kissinger, *Special Adviser*, CFR/TC
David Rockefeller, *Special Adviser*, CFR/TC
T. Tannenwald, Jr., *U.S. Tax Court*, CFR
Abbott Washburn, *Federal Communications Commission*, CFR
George Dalley, *Civil Aeronautics Board*, CFR
James Duffy, *Postal Rate Commission*, CFR
Adm. Bobby Inman, *Deputy Director, CIA*, CFR
J.R. West, *Asst. to Secretary of the Interior*, CFR
Bruce Babbitt, *Adv. Commission on Intergovernmental Relations*, CFR
William Brock, Jr., *Special Trade Representative*, CFR/TC

Eleanor Norton, *National Commission for Employment Policy*, CFR
Willard Butcher, *President's Commission on Executive Exchange*, CFR/TC
Thornton Bradshaw, *President's Commission on Executive Exchange*, CFR
John McKinley, *President's Commission on Executive Exchange*, CFR
Ruben Mettler, *President's Commission on Executive Exchange*, CFR
John Whitehead, *President's Commission on Executive Exchange*, CFR
Marina V.N. Whitman, *President's Commission on Executive Exchange*, CFR/TC

Department of State

George P. Schultz, *Secretary*, CFR
Walter Stoessel, Jr., *Under Secretary*, CFR
Carol Bauman, *Research*, CFR
Richard Burt, *Politico Military Affairs*, CFR
Mark Feldman, *Legal*, CFR
Ann Hollick, *Policy Assessment*, CFR
Robert Hormats, *Economics, Business*, CFR
Edward Morse, *Internal Energy Policy*, CFR
Michael Peacy, *Legal, Law Enforcement*, CFR
Raymond Platig, *Intelligence, Research*, CFR
Myer Rashish, *Economic Affairs*, CFR
Paul Wolfowitz, *Policy Planning*, CFR
James Spain, *Administration*, CFR
Luigi Einaudi, *Bureau of Inter-American Affairs*, CFR
Chester Crocker, *Bureau of African Affairs*, CFR

Michael Armacost, *Bureau of East Asian & Pacific Affairs*, CFR
Frederick Brown, *Bureau of East Asian & Pacific Affairs*, CFR
John Negroponte, *Bureau of East Asian & Pacific Affairs*, CFR
Lawrence Eagleburger, *Bureau of European Affairs*, CFR
Sandra Vogelgesang, *Bureau of European Affairs*, CFR
Elliott Abrams, *Bureau of International Organiztion Affairs*, CFR

Ambassadors

Jeane Kirkpatrick, *United Nations*, CFR
Richard Petree, *United Nations*, CFR
Morton Abramowitz, *Thailand*, CFR
Michael Armacost, *Philippines*, CFR
Alfred Atherton, *Egypt*, CFR
Harry Barnes, Jr., *India*, CFR
Harry Bergold, Jr., *Hungary*, CFR
Richard Blomfield, *Portugal*, CFR
Charles Bray, III, *Senegal*, CFR
Arthur Burns, *West Germany*, CFR
Horace Dawson, *Botswana*, CFR
Angier Duke, *Morocco*, CFR
James E. Goodby, *Finland*, CFR
Arthur Hartman, *U.S.S.R.*, CFR
Deane Hinton, *El Salvador*, CFR
Samuel Lewis, *Israel*, CFR
James Lowenstein, *Luxembourg*, CFR
William Luers, *Venezuela*, CFR
Ronald Palmer, *Malaysia*, CFR
Thomas Pickering, *Nigeria*, CFR
Maxwell Rabb, *Italy*, CFR
Ronald Spiers, *Pakistan*, CFR
R. Stausz-Hupe, *Turkey*, CFR
Terence Todman, *Spain*, CFR

CFR/TC Connections In The Congress

U.S. Senate (Current or Recent)
Howard Baker, *Tennessee*, CFR
Birch Bayh, *Indiana*, CFR
Lloyd Bentsen, *Texas*, CFR
William Brock, *Tennessee*, CFR/TC
Edward Brooke, *Massachusetts*, CFR
Clifford Case, *New Jesery*, CFR
Frank Church, *Idaho*, CFR

Dick Clark, *Iowa*, CFR
William S. Cohen, *Maine*, CFR/TC
Alan Cranston, *California*, TC
John Cooper, *Kentucky*, CFR
John Culver, *Iowa*, CFR/TC
John Danforth, *Missouri*, TC
John Glenn, *Ohio*, TC
Jacob Javits, *New York*, CFR
Ted Kennedy, *Massachusetts*, CFR
   (belongs to Boston Affiliate)
Gale McGee, *Wyoming*, CFR
George McGovern, *South Dakota*, CFR
Charles Mathias, *Maryland*, CFR
Walter Mondale, *Minnesota*, CFR/TC
Daniel Moynihan, *New York*, CFR
Edmund Muskie, *Maine*, CFR
Claiborne Pell, *Rhode Island*, CFR
Abraham Ribicoff, *Connecticut*, CFR
William Roth, *Delaware*, CFR/TC
Paul Sarbanes, *Maryland*, CFR
Adlai Stevenson, *Illinois*, CFR
Stuart Symington, *Missouri*, CFR
Robert Taft, Jr., *Ohio*, TC

House of Representatives

John Anderson, *Illinois*, CFR/TC
Les Aspin, *Wisconsin*, CFR
J.B. Bingham, *New York*, CFR
John Brademas, *Indiana*, CFR/TC
Barber Conable, Jr., *New York*, TC
William R. Cotter, *Conecticut*, CFR
Dante Fascell, *Florida*, CFR
Thomas Foley, *Washington*, TC
Donald Fraser, *New York*, CFR/TC
James R. Jones, *Oklahoma*, TC
Charles Schumer, *New York*, CFR
Stephen Solarz, *New York*, CFR

The Media

CBS
William Paley, CFR
William Burden, CFR
Roswell Gilpatric, CFR
James Houghton, CFR
Henry Schacht, CFR/TC
Marietta Tree, CFR
Charles C. Collingwood, CFR
Lawrence LeSueun, CFR
Dan Rather, CFR

Harry Reasoner, CFR
Richart C. Hottelet, CFR
Frank Stanton, CFR
Bill Moyer, CFR

NBC/RCA
Jane Pfeiffer, CFR
Lester Crystal, CFR
R.W. Sonnenfeldt, CFR
T.F. Bradshaw, CFR
John Petty, CFR
David Brinkley, CFR
John Chancellor, CFR
Marvin Kalb, CFR
Irvine Levine, CFR
H. Schlosser, CFR
P.G. Peterson, CFR/TC
John Sawhill, CFR/TC

ABC
Ray Adam, CFR
Frank Cary, CFR
John Connor, CFR
T.M. Macioce, CFR
Ted Coppell, CFR
John Scale, CFR
Barbara Walters, CFR

Cable News Network
Daniel Schorr, CFR

Public Broadcasting System
Hartford Gunn, CFR
Robert McNeil, CFR
Jim Lehrer, CFR
C. Hunter-Gault, CFR
Hodding Carter, CFR

Associated Press
Keith Fuller, CFR
Stanley Swinton, CFR
Louis Boccardi, CFR
Harold Anderson, CFR
Katharine Graham, CFR

United Press International
H.L. Stevenson, CFR

Reuters
Michael Posner, CFR

Boston Globe
David Rogers, CFR

L.A. Times Syndicate
Joseph Kraft, CFR

Baltimore Sun
Henry Trewhitt, CFR

New York Times Company
Richard Gelb, CFR
James Reston, CFR
William Scranton, CFR/TC
A. M. Rosentahal, CFR
Seymour Topping, CFR
James Greenfield, CFR
Max Frankel, CFR
Jack Rosenthal, CFR
Harding Bancroft, CFR
Amory Bradford, CFR
Orvil Dryfoos, CFR
David Halberstram, CFR
Walter Lippmann, CFR
L.E. Markel, CFR
H.L. Mathews, CFR
John Oakes, CFR
Adolph Ochs, CFR
Harrison Salisbury, CFR
A. Hays Sulzberger, CFR
A. Ochs Sulzberger, CFR
G.L. Sulzberger, CFR
H.L. Smith, CFR
Steven Rattner, CFR
Richard Burt, CFR

Time, Inc.
Ralph Davidson, CFR
Daonal M. Wilson, CFR
Louis Banks, CFR
Henry Grunwald, CFR
Alexander Heard, CFR
Sol Linowitz, CFR/TC
Rawleigh Warner, Jr., CFR
Thomas Watson, Jr., CFR

Newsweek/Washington Post
Katharine Graham, CFR
Philip Graham, CFR
Arjay Miller, TC

158

Nicholas deB. Katzenbach, CFR
Frederick Beebe, CFR
Robert Christopher, CFR
A. De Borchgrave, CFR
Osborne Elliot, CFR
Phillip Geyelin, CFR
Kermit Lausen, CFR
Murry Marder, CFR
Eugene Meyer, CFR
Malcolm Muir, CFR
Maynard Parker, CFR
George Will, CFR
Robert Kaiser, CFR
Meg Greenfield, CFR
Walter Pincus, CFR
Murray Gart, CFR
Peter Osnos, CFR
Don Oberdorfer, CFR

Dow Jones Co.
(Wall Street Journal)
William Agee, CFR
J. Paul Austin, TC
Charles Meyer, CFR
Robert Potter, CFR
Richard Wood, CFR
Robert Bartley, CFR
Karen House, CFR

National Review
William F. Buckley, Jr., CFR
Richard Brookhiser, CFR

The Banking Establishment

Paul Volcker, *Chairman, Federal Reserve Bank*, CFR
Robert McNamara, *Chairman, International Bank for Reconstruction & Development*, CFR
Donald Regan, *Secretary of the Treasury*, CFR
W.B. Dale, *International Monetary Fund*, CFR
H.B. Chenery, *World Bank*, CFR

Chase Manhattan Corp.
David Rockefeller, CFR/TC

Willard C. Butcher, CFR
William S. Ogden, CFR
Robert R. Douglass, CFR
John C. Haley, CFR
Charles F. Barber, CFR
J.R. Dilworth, CFR
Richard M. Furlaud, CFR
Theodore Hesburgh, CFR
Ralph Lazarus, CFR
Edmund T. Pratt, Jr., CFR
S. Bruce Smart, Jr., CFR
William T. Coleman, Jr., CFR/TC
James L. Ferguson, CFR
Alexander Haig, Jr., CFR
John D. Macomber, CFR
Leo Martinuzzi, Jr., CFR
Franklin Wiliams, CFR
John D. Wilson, CFR

Bankers Trust Company
Alfred Brittain, III, CFR
David O. Beim, CFR
Carlos Canal, Jr., CFR
Richard L. Gelb, CFR
Calvin H. Plimpton, CFR
Patricia Stewart, CFR
John W. Brooks, CFR
Vernon Jordan, Jr., CFR
William Tavoulareas, CFR

Morgan Guaranty
Lewis T. Preston, CFR
Alexander Vagliano, CFR
Rimmer de Vries, CFR
Jackson B. Gilbert, CFR
Ray C. Adam, CFR
Carter L. Burgess, CFR
Frank T. Cary, CFR
Emilio G. Colladoicfr
Alan Greenspan, CFR
Howard Johnson, CFR
James L. Ketelsen, CFR
Walter H. Page, CFR
Ellmore Patterson, CFR
J. Paul Austin, TC

Chemical Bank
Donald C. Platten, CFR
Charles Carson, Jr., CFR

Richard LeBlond, II, CFR
Walter V. Shipley, CFR
Robert J. Callander, CFR
Frederick L. Deming, CFR

First National of Chicago
William McDonough, CFR
Robert S. Ingersoll, CFR/TC
Brooks McCormick, CFR
Lee L. Morgan, CFR

Manufacturers Hanover .
Charles J. Pilliod, Jr., CFR

Citibank
Walter B. Wriston, CFR
G. A. Costanzo, CFR
Hans Angerlmueller, CFR
George J. Vojta, CFR
Lief H. Olsen, CFR
Thomas Theobald, CFR

The Business Establishment

Exxon/Standard
Clifton Gavin, Jr., CFR
Jack Bennett, CFR
W. Bromery, CFR
J.G. Clark, CFR
J.E. Dean, CFR
J.K. Jamieson, CFR
Franklin Long, CFR
George Percy, CFR
Otto von Amerongen, TC
Stephen Stamas, CFR
J.A. Armstrong, CFR
George M. Keller, CFR
Carla Hills, TC
David Packard, TC
Charles M. Pigott, CFR
George Weyerhaeuser, TC

Mobil
Raleigh Warner, Jr., CFR
William Tavoulareas, CFR
Lewis Branscomb, CFR
Howard L. Clark, CFR
Alan Greenspan, CFR

George McGhee, CFR
Lee L. Morgan, CFR/TC
Herbert Schmertz, CFR
Eleanor B. Sheldon, CFR

Atlantic Richfield
Robert O. Anderson, CFR
T.F. Bradshaw, CFR
Philip M. Hawley, TC
Robert Ingersoll, CFR
John B. M. Place, CFR
Frank Stanton, CFR

Texaco
Maurice F. Granville, CFR
John K. McKinley, CFR
Robert V. Roosa, CFR/TC

Gulf
James E. Lee, CFR

Shell
John F. Bookout, CFR

Occidental
A. Robert Abboud, CFR

General Electric
Reginald H. Jones, CFR
John F. Burlingame, TC

AT&T
Edward W. Carter, CFR
Jerome H. Hollard, CFR
Juanita M. Kreps, CFR
Peter E. Haas, CFR
William A. Hewitt, CFR/TC
Rawleigh Warner, Jr. , CFR

Caterpillar
L.L. Morgan, CFR
Ralph S. Ingersoll, CFR/TC

John Deere
William A. Hewitt, CFE/TC

Texas Instruments
Mark Shepherd, Jr., CFR/TC
J. Fred Bucy, Jr., CFR

Chrysler Corp.
Jerome Holland, CFR
Najeeb Halaby, CFR
Tom Killefer, CFR
J. R. Dilworth, CFR
Gabriel Hauge, CFR

General Motors
Reuben R. Jensen, CFR
Roger B. Smith, CFR
Marina N. Whitman, CFR/TC

Ford Motor Company
Donald E. Peterson, CFR
Carter L. Burgess, CFR
Clifton Wharton, Jr., CFR
Philip Caldwell, TC
Arjay Miller, TC

**The Labor
Establishment**
I.W. Abel, *former President, United Steel-
workers of America,* TC
Sol Chaiken, *President, International*

Ladies' Garment Workers, CFR/TC
Thomas R. Bonahue, *Secretary/Treasurer,
AFL-CIO,* CFR/TC
Murray H. Finley, *President, Amalgam-
ated Clothing & Textile Workers,* CFR
Victor Gotbaum, *American Federation
of State, County & Municipal
Workers,* CFR
Lane Kirkland, *President,
AFL-CIO,* CFR/TC
Howard D. Samuel, *President, Industrial
Union Department, AFL-CIO,* CFR
Martin J. Ward, *President, United Assn.
of Journeymen & Apprentices of the
Plumbing and Pipe Fitting
Industry,* CFR/TC
Glenn E. Watts, *President, Communication
Workers of America,* CFR/TC
Leonard Woodcock, *former President,
United Auto Workers, first Ambassador
to Communist China,* CFR/TC
Jerry Wurf, *President, American Federa-
tion of State, County & Municipal
Employees,* CFR

PLEASE NOTE

The above listings are merely representative of the vast power and influence that members of the Council on Foreign Relations and the Trilateral Commission possess. Space limitations prevent us from including many other banking, business, and government connections — not to mention the colleges, universities, and tax-free foundations controlled by the "Insiders."

We are indebted to Johnny Stewart of F.R.E.E. in Waco, Texas, for the work he has done since the original publication of *None Dare Call It Conspiracy,* in charting the CFR/TC connections of many "Insiders."

F.R.E.E. has published a series of charts and pamphlets that are invaluable in showing the CFR/TC connections. For a package of information, please send $5.00 (for postage and handling) to:

Johnny Stewart
F.R.E.E.
P.O. Box 8616
Waco, Texas 76710

Appendix II

COUNCIL ON FOREIGN RELATIONS

Membership Roster
As of June 30, 1982

A

Aaron, David L.
Abboud. A Robert
Abegglen, James C.
Abel, Elie
Abely, Joseph F., Jr.
Abram, Morris B.
Abromowitz, Morton I.
Abrams, Elliott
Abshire, David M.
Achilles, Theodore C.
Adam, Ray C.
Adams, Ruth Salzman
Admson, David
Agee, William M.
Agnew, William M.
Agnew, Harold M.
Aidinoff, M. Bernard
Atkins, James E.
Albert, Judith D.
Albright, Archie E.
Albright, Madeleine
Alderman, Michael H.
Aldrich, George H.
Alexander, Robert J.
Alibrandi, Joseph F.
Allan, F. Aley
Allbrition, Joe L.
Allen, Lew Jr.
Allen, Philip E.
Allen, Raymond B.
Allen, Robert H.
Alley, James B.
Allison, Graham T.
Allison, Richard C.
Allport Alexander W.
Alpern, Alan N.
Altman, Roiger C.
Altschul, Arthur G.
Andersen, Harold W.

Anderson, John B.
Anderson, Robert
Anderson, Robert B.
Anderson, Robert O.
Anderson, Roy A.
Angell, James W.
Angermueller, Hans H.
Angulo, Manuel R.
Anschuetz, Norbert L.
Anthoine, Robert
Apter, David E.
Araskog, Rand V.
Arledge, Roone
Armacost, Michael H.
Armacost, Samuel H.
Armstrong, Anne
Armstrong, C. M.
Armstrong, DeWitt C., III
Armstrong, John A.
Armstrong, Willis C.
Arnold, Millard W.
Aron, Adam M.
Art, Robert J.
Asencio, Diego C.
Asher, Robert E.
Askew, Reuben O'D.
Aspin, Les
Assousa, George E.
Atherton, Alfred L., Jr.
Atkins, Charles Agee
Attwood, William
Auspitz, Josiah Lee

B

Babbitt, Bruce
Bacot, J. Carter
Bader, William B.
Baeza, MarioL.
Bailey, Charles W.
Baird, Zoe E.

Baker, Howard H., Jr.
Baker, James E.
Baker, Pauline H.
Baldrige, Malcolm
Baldwin, Robert E.
Baldwin, Robert H. B.
Bales, Carter F.
Ball, David George
Ball, George W.
Ballou, George T.
Bancroft, Harding F.
Banks, Louis L.
Barber, Charles F.
Barber, Joseph
Barber, Perry O., Jr.
Barger, Thomas C.
Barghoorn, Frederick C.
Barker, Robert R.
Barkin, Solomon
Barlow, William E.
Barnds, William J.
Barnes, Harry G., Jr.
Barnes, Michael D.
Barnet Richard J.
Barnett, A. Doak
Barnett, Frank R.
Barnett, Robert W.
Barrand, Harry P., Jr.
Barrett, Edward W.
Barron, Deborah Durfee
Barrows, Leland
Batholomew, Reginald
Bartlett, Joseph W.
Bartlett, Thomas A.
Bartley, Robert L.
Bassow, Whitman
Bastedo, Phillip
Batkin, Alan R.
Bator, Francis M.
Bator, Peter A.
Battle, Lucius D.

Bauman, Robert P.
Baumann, Carol Edler
Bayne, Edward Ashley
Beam, Jacob D.
Bean, Atherton
Bechtel, S. D.
Becker, E. Lovell
Beckler, David Z.
Beeman, Richard E.
Begley, Louis
Behrman, Jack N.
Beim, David O.
Beinecke, William S.
Bell, Daniel
Bell, David E.
Bell, Holey Mack
Bell, J. Bowyer
Bell, Peter D.
Bell, Travers J., Jr.
Bellamy, Carol
Benbow, Terence H.
Bennet, Douglas J., Jr.
Bennett, Donald V.
Bennett, J. F.
Bennett, W. Tapley, Jr.
Benson, Lucy Wilson
Beplat, Tristan E.
Berger, Marilyn
Berger, Peter L.
Berger, Suzanne
Bergold, Harry E., Jr.
Bergsten, C. Fred
Berman, Maureen R.
Berstein, Robert L.
Berry, Sidney B.
Bessie, Simon Michael
Betts, Richard K.
Bialer, Seweryn
Bienen, Henry S.
Bierley, John C.
Billington, James H.
Binger, James H.
Bingham, Jonathan B.
Birkelund, John P.
Bisnow, Mark C.
Bissell, Richard E.
Bissell, Richard M., Jr.
Black, Cyril E.
Black, Edwin F.

Black, Joseph E.
Black, Leon D.
Black, Shirley Temple
Blackmer, Donald L. M.
Blake, Robert O.
Blake, Vaughn R.
Blank, Stephen
Blechman, Barry M.
Blendon, Robert J.
Bliss, Richard M.
Bloch, Henry Simon
Bloomfield, Lincoln P.
Bloomfield, Richard J.
Blum, John A.
Blumenthal, W. Michael
Boardman, Harry
Boccardi, Louis D.
Bodine, William W., Jr.
Boeschenstein, William W.
Bogdan, Norbert A.
Boggs, Michael D.
Bohen, Frederick M.
Boling, Landrum R.
Bond, Robert D.
Bonney, J. Dennis
Bonsal, Dudley B.
Bonsal, Philip W.
Bookout, John F.
Boorman, Howard L.
Borton, Hugh
Bower, Joseph L.
Bowie, Robert R.
Bowles, Chester
Bowman, Richard C.
Boyd, William M., II
Boyer, Ernest L.
Brademas, John
Bradford, Zeb B., Jr.
Bradley, William L.
Bradshaw, Thornton F.
Braisted, Paul J.
Branscomb, Lewis M.
Branson, William H.
Bray, Charles W., III
Breck, Henry Reynolds
Breindel, Eric M.
Bresnan, John J.
Brewster, Kingman
Brimmer, Andrew F.

Brinkley, David
Brinkley, George A.
Brittain, Alfred, III
Brittenham, Raymond L.
Brock, Mitchell
Brock, William E., III
Brockway, George P.
Broda, Frederick C.
Bromery, Randolph Wilson
Bronfman, Edgar M.
Vronwell, Arthur
Brooke, Edward W.
Brookhiser, Richard S.
Brooks, Harvey
Brooks, John W.
Brorby, Melvin
Bross, John A.
Brower, Charles N.
Brown, Frederic J.
Brown, Harold
Brown, Harrison Scott
Brown, Irving
Brown, L. Dean
Brown, Lester R.
Brown, Richard P., Jr.
Brown, Seyom
Brown, Walter H.
Browne, Robert S.
Bruce, Judith
Bryant, Ralph C.
Brzezinski, Zbigniew
Buchman, Mark E.
Buckley, William F., Jr.
Bucy, J. Fred, Jr.
Bullitt, John C.
Bullock, Hugh
Bullock, Mary Brown
Bundy, McGeorge
Bundy, William P.
Bunker, Carol Laise
Bunker, Ellsworth
Buynnell, C. Sterling
Bunting, John R.
Burden, William A. M.
Burgess, Carter L.
Burns, Arthur F.
Burns, Patrick Owen
Burt, Richard R.
Bush, Donald F.

Bushner, Rolland H.
Bussey, Donald S.
Butcher, Goler Teal
Butcher, Willard C.
Butler, Samuel C.
Butler, William J.
Buttenwieser, Benjamin J.
Byrnes, Robert F.
Byrom, Fletcher

C

Cabot, Louis W.
Cabot, Thomas D.
Cabranes, Jose A.
Calder, Alexander, Jr.
Califano, Joseph A., Jr.
Calkins, Hugh
Callander, Robert J.
Calleo, David P.
Campbell, Glenn
Campbell, John C.
Campbell, Thomas J.
Camps, Miriam
Canal, Carlos M., Jr.
Canfield, Cass
Canfield, Franklin O.
Cannon, James M.
Carey, Hugh L.
Carey, John
Carlucci, Frank C.
Carmichael, William D.
Carnesale, Albert
Carrington, Walter C.
Carroll, J. Speed
Carroll, Mitchell B.
Carson, C. W., Jr.
Carter, Barry E.
Carter, Edward William
Carter, Hodding, III
Carter, Robert L.
Carter, William D.
Cary, Frank T.
Cary, William L.
Case, John C.
Casey, William J.
Cater, Douglass
Cater, John T.
Cates, John M., Jr.

Catto, Henry E. Jr.
Chace, James
Chafee, John H.
Chaikin, Sol Chick
Challenor, Herschelle S.
Chancellor, John
Changler, George A.
Chapman, John F.
Charpie, Robert A.
Chase, W. Howard
Chayes, Abram J.
Chayes, Antonia Handler
Cheever, Daniel S.
Chen, Kimball C.
Chenery, Hollis B.
Cheney, Richard B.
Cherne, Leo
Chickering, A. Lawrence
Childs, Marquis W.
Chira, Susan D.
Chittenden, George H.
Christopher, Robert C.
Christopher, Warren M.
Chubb, Hendon
Church, Edgar M.
Cisler, Walker L.
Cisnerous, Henry G.
Clapp, Priscilla A.
Clark, Bronson P.
Clark, Dick
Clark, Howard L.
Clark, Kenneth B.
Clark, Ralph L.
Clarke, J. G.
Cleveland, Harlan
Cleveland, Harold van B.
Clifford, Donald K., Jr.
Cline, Ray S.
Clurman, Richard M.
Cochetti, Roger J.
Coffey, Joseph Irving
Cohen, Benjamin J.
Cohen, Benjamin V.
Cohen, Jerome Alan
Cohen, Jerome B.
Cohen, Joel E.
Cohen, Roberta
Cohen, Stephen B.
Cohen, Stephen F.

Cohen, William S.
Colby, William E.
Coleman, James S.
Coleman, William T., Jr.
Coles, James Stacy
Collado, Emilio G.
Collingwood, Charles C.
Combs, Richard E., Jr.
Comstock, Phil
Conant, Melvin A.
Condon, Joseph F.
Cone, Sydney M., III
Conlon, Richard P.
Connor, John T.
Connor, John T., Jr.
Connor, Joseph E.
Connor, Kristen R.
Conway, Jill
Cook, Gary M.
Cook, Howard A.
Cooley, Richard P.
Coolidge, Nicholas J.
Coolidge, T. J., Jr.
Coombs, Philip H.
Cooney, Joan Ganz
Cooper, Charles A.
Coioper, Chester L.
Cooper, Richard N.
Copeland, Lammot du Pont
Corrigan, Kevin
Cott, Suzanne
Cotter, Wiliam R.
Cousins, Norman
Cowan, L. Gray
Cowles, Gardner
Cowles, John, Jr.
Cox, Robert G.
Craig, Earl D., Jr.
Crane, Winthrop Murray
Crassweller, Robert D.
Creel, Dana S.
Crittenden, Ann
Crocker, Chester A.
Crook, William H.
Crosby, Ralph D., Jr.
Crow, Trammell
Crowe, William J., Jr.
Crystal, Lester M.
Culver, John C.

165

Cummings, Robert L.
Cummiskey, Frank J.
Curtis, Gerald L.
Cusick, Peter
Cutler, Lloyd N.
Cutler, Walter L.
Cutter, W. Bowman
Cyr, Arthur

D

Dale, William B.
Dalley, George A.
Dallin, Alexander
Dam, Kenneth W.
Damrosch, Lori F.
Daniel, D. Ronald
Darlington, Charles F.
Darman, Richard G.
Darrell, Norris
Davant, James W.
Davidson, Daniel I.
Davidson, Ralph K.
Davidson, Ralph P.
Davis, John A.
Davis, Lynn E.
Davis, Nathaniel
Davis, Vincent
Davison, Daniel P.
Davison, W. Phillips
Dawkins, Peter M.
Dawson, Horace G., Jr.
Day Arthur R.
Deagle, Edwin A., Jr.
Dean, Arthur H.
Dean, Jonathan
Debevoise, Eli Whitney
Debevoise, Eli Whitney, II
De Borchgrave, Arnaud
Debs, Richard A.
Decter, Midge
De Cubas, Jose
Dee, Robert F.
Dees, Bowen C.
De Janosi, Peter E.
De Kiewiet, C. W.
De Lima, Oscar A.
De Menil, Lois Pattison
Deming, Frederick L.

DeMuth, Christopher C.
Denison, Robert J.
Dennard, Cleveland L.
Dennison, Charles S.
Denton, E. Hazel
DePalma, Samuel
De Rosso, Alphonse
Destler, I. M.
Deutch, Michael J.
Devine, C. Robert
Devine, Thomas J.
DeVries, Henry P.
DeVries, Rimmer
DeWind, Adrian W.
DeWindt, E. Mandell
Dia Alejandro, Carlos F.
Dickey, John Sloan
Dickson, R. Russell, Jr.
Diebold, John
Diebold, William, Jr.
Dietel, William M.
Dil, Shaheen F.
Dilon, Douglas
Dilworth, J. Richardson
Dine, Thomas A.
Dixon, George H.
Dodge, Cleveland E.
Doherty, William C., Jr.
Dolin, Arnold
Dominguez, Jorge I.
Dominguez, Virginia R.
Donahue, Donald J.
Donahue, Thomas R.
Donaldson, William H.
Donnell, Ellsworth
Donelly, Harold C.
Donovan, Hedley
Doty, Paul M., Jr.
Douce, Wm. C.
Douglas, Paul W.
Douglass, Robert R.
Draper, Theodore
Dreier, John C.
Drell, Sidney D.
Drew, Elizabeth
Drumwright, J. R.
Dubow, Arthur M.
DuBrul, Stephen M.
Duffey, Joseph

Duffy, James H.
Duke, Angier Biddle
Duncan, Charles W., Jr.
Duncan, John C.
Dungan, Ralph A.
Dutton, Frederick G.
Raoul-Duval, Michael
Dyke, Nancy Bearg

E

Eagleburger, Lawrence S.
Earle, Ralph, II
Easum, Donald B.
Eaton, David J.
Eaton, Leonard J., Jr.
Eberle, William D.
Eckholm, Erik P.
Edelman, Alber I.
Edelman, Gerald M.
Edelman, Marian Wright
Edelstein, Julius C. C.
Edgerton, Wallace B.
Edwards, Howard L.
Edwards, Robert H.
Ehrlich, Thomas
Eilts, Hermann F.
Einaudi, Luigi R.
Einaudi, Mario
Einhorn, Jessica P.
Eliot, Theodore L., Jr.
Elliott, Byron K.
Elliott, Osborn
Elliott, Randle
Ellis, James R.
Elison, Keith P.
Ellsberg, Daniel
Ellsworth, Robert F.
Embree, Ainslie T.
Enders, Thomas Ostrom
Eng, Gordon
Enthoven, Alain
Epstein, Jason
Epstein, Joshua M.
Erb, Gay F.
Erb, Richard D.
Erbsen, Claude E.
Erburu, Robert F.
Estabrook, Robert H.

Etzioni, Amitai
Evans, John C.
Evans, John K.
Ewing, William, Jr.
Exter, John

F

Fabian, Larry L.
Fairbank, John King
Fairbanks, Douglas
Falk, Richard A.
Farer, Tom J.
Farmer, Thomas L.
Fascell, Dante B.
Feer, Mark C.
Feiner, Ava S.
Feith, Douglas J.
Feldman, Mark B.
Feldstein, Martin S.
Fenster, Steven R.
Ferguson, C. Clyde, Jr.
Ferguson, Glenn W.
Ferguson, James L.
Ferre, Maurice A.
Fessenden, Hart
Field, Robert E.
Fierce, Milfred C.
Fifield, Russell H.
Filer, John H.
Finger, Seymour M.
Finkelstein, Lawrence S.
Finley, Murray H.
Finn, James
Finney, Paul B.
Firmage, Edwin B.
Fisher, Adrian S.
Fisher, Peter A.
Fisher, Richard W.
Fisher, Roger
Fishlow, Albert
FitzGerald, Frances
Fitzgibbons, Harold E.
Flanigan, Peter M.
Fleck, G. Peter
Foley, S. R., Jr.
Foote, Edward T., Jr.
Ford, Gerald R.
Forrestal, Michael V.

Foster, William C.
Fousek, Peter
Fowler, Henry H.
Fox, Donald T.
Fox, Joseph C.
Fox, William T. R.
Franck, Thomas M.
Francke, Albert, III
Frank, Charles R., Jr.
Frank, Isaiah
Frank, Richard A.
Frankel, Francine R.
Frankel, Max
Franklin, George S.
Fraser, Donald M.
Frederick, Pauline
Fredericks, J. Wayne
Freeman, Orville L.
Frelinghuysen, Peter H. B.
French, John
Freund, Gerald
Frey, Donald N.
Freytag, Richard A.
Fribourg, Michel
Fried, Edward R.
Friedman, Benjamin M.
Friedman, Irving S.
Friele, Berent
Friendly, Henry J.
Fromkin, David
Frost, F. Daniel
Frye, Alton
Frye, William R.
Fuerbringer, Otto
Fukuyama, Francis
Fuller, Keith
Funari, John
Funkhouser, E. N., Jr.
Furlaud, Richard M.
Fuzesi, Stephen, Jr.
Fye, Paul M.

G

Galbraith, Evan G.
Gallatin, James P.
Ganoe, Charles S.
Gard, Robert G., Jr.
Gardner, Richard N.

Garment, Leonard
Garment, Suzanne
Garretson, Albert H.
Garrett, David C., Jr.
Garrison, Mark J.
Gart, Murray H.
Garthoff, Raymond L.
Garvin, Clifton C., Jr.
Garvy, George
Garwin, Richard L.
Gates, Thomas S.
Gati, Charles
Gati, Toby Trister
Geertz, Clifford
Geiger, Theodore
Gelb, Leslie H.
Gelb, Richard L.
Gell-Mann, Murray
George, Alexander L.
George, W. H. Krome
Gerson, Elliot F.
Gerstner, Louis V., Jr.
Geyelin, Henry R.
Geyelin, Philip L.
Giamatti, A. Bartlett
Gibney, Frank B.
Giffen, James H.
Gil, Peter P.
Gilbert, H. N.
Gilbert, Jackson B.
Gilbert, Jarobin, Jr.
Gillespie, S. Hazard
Gilmore, Kenneth O.
Gilpatric, Roswell L.
Gilpin, Robert
Ginsburg, David
Ginsburg, Ruth Bader
Binsburgh, Robert N.
Gleysteen, Peter
Globerman, Norman
Glushien, Ruth N.
Godchaux, Frank A., III
Goekjian, Samuel V.
Gogel, Donald Jay
Goheen, Robert F.
Goizueta, Roberto C.
Goldberg, Marvin L.
Golden, William T.
Goldin, Harrison J.

Goldman, Guido
Goldman, Marshall I.
Goldman, Merle
Goldmark, Peter C., Jr.
Goldsborough, James O.
Goldschmidt, Neil
Gompert, David C.
Good, Robert C.
Goodby, James E.
Goodman, George J. W.
Goodman, Herbert I.
Goodpaster, Andrew J.
Goodsell, James Nelson
Gordon, Albert H.
Gordon, Lincoln
Gordon, Michael R.
Gorman, Paul F.
Gornick, Alan L.
Gotbaum, Victor
Gould, Peter G.
Gousseland, Pierre
Grace, J. Peter
Graff, Henry F.
Graff, Robert D.
Graham, Bob
Graham, Katharine
Grant, James P.
Grant, Stephen A.
Granville, Maurice F.
Graubard, Stephen R.
Grayson, Bruns H.
Greenberg, Maurice R.
Greenberg, Sanford D.
Greene, James C.
Greene, James R.
Greene, Joseph N., Jr.
Greene, Margaret L.
Greenfield, James L.
Greenfield, Meg
Greenhill, Robert F.
Greenough, William C.
Greenspan, Alan
Greenwald, Joseph A.
Greenwood, Ted
Griffin, Brian C.
Griffith, Thomas
Griffith, William E.
Grohman, Robert T.
Grose, Peter B.

Gross, Ernest A.
Gross, Patrick W.
Groves, Ray J.
Grunwald, Henry A.
Gullion, Edmund A.
Gulliver, Adelaide Cromwell
Gunn, Hartford N., Jr.
Gutfreund, John H.
Guthman, Edwin O.
Gwertzman, Bernard M.
Gwin, Catherine B.

H

Haas, Peter E.
Haass, Richard N.
Habib, Philip C.
Haig, Alexander M., Jr.
Haight, G. Winthrop
Halaby, Najeeb E.
Hale, Roger L.
Haley, John C.
Hallingby, Paul, Jr.
Halperin, Morton H.
Halsted, Thomas A.
Hamilton, Ann O.
Hamilton, Charles V.
Hamilton, Edward K.
Hamilton, Fowler
Hamilton, Michael P.
Hansen, Roger D.
Hanson, Thor
Harari, Maurice
Harbin, John P.
Harding, Harry
Hare, Raymond A.
Hargrove, John Lawrence
Harpel, James W.
Harper, Conrad K.
Harper, Paul C., Jr.
Harriman, W. Averell
Harris, Irving B.
Harris, Joseph E.
Harris, Patricia Roberts
Harrison, Selig S.
Harsch, Joseph C.
Hart, Augustin S., Jr.
Hart, Parker T.
Hartley, Fred L.

Hartman, Arthur A.
Hartnack, Carl E.
Harvin, Wiliam C.
Haskell, John H. F., Jr.
Haskins, Caryl P.
Hauge, John R.
Hauser, Rita E.
Hauser, William L.
Haviland, H. Field, Jr.
Hawkins, Ashton
Hayes, Alfred
Hayes, Samuel P.
Haynes, Fred
Haynes, Ulric St. C., Jr.
Haywood, Oliver G.
Hazard, John N.
Healy, Harold H., Jr.
Heard, Alexander
Heck, Charles B.
Heckscher, August
Hehir, J. Bryan
Heifetz, Elaine F.
Heimann, John G.
Heintzen, Harry L.
Heinz, H. J. II
Helander, Robert C.
Heldring, Frederick
Hellman, F. Warren
Helms, Christine M.
Helms, Richard
Henderson, James B.
Henderson, Lawrence J., Jr.
Henderson, Loy W.
Henderson, William
Henkin, Louis
Hennessy, John M.
Henry, John B., II
Heling, John
Herskovits, Jean
Hertrer, Christian A., Jr.
Hertzberg, Arthur
Herzfeld, Charles M.
Herzog, Paul M.
Herzstein, Robert E.
Hesburgh, Theodore M.
Hester, James M.
Hewitt, William A.
Heyns, Roger W.
Hickey, William M.

Highet, Keith
Hillenbrand, Martin J.
Hilsman, Roger
Hines, Gerald D.
Hinshaw, Randall
Hinton, Deane R.
Hirschman, Albert O.
Hoagland, Jim
Hobby, William P.
Hoch, Frank W.
Hochschild, Walter
Hodgson, James D.
Hodin, Michael W.
Hoffman, Michael L.
Hoffmann, Stanley
Hoge, James
Hoguet, George R.
Hoguet, Robert L.
Hohenberg, John
Holbrooke, Richard C.
Holcomb, M. Staser
Holland, Jerome H.
Holland, Robert C.
Hollick, Ann L.
Holloway, Anne F.
Holmes, Alan R.
Holst, Willem
Holt, Pat M.
Homer, Sidney
Hooks, Benjamin L.
Hoopes, Townsend W.
Hoover, Herbert W., Jr.
Horan, John J.
Horelick, Arnold L.
Hormats, Robert D.
Horn, Garfield H.
Horowitz, Irving Louis
Horton, Alan W.
Horton, Philip C.
Hosmer, Bradley C.
Hoston, Germaine A.
Hottelet, Richard C.
Houghton, Amory, Jr.
Houghton, Arthur A., Jr.
Houghton, James R.
House, Karen Elliott
Hovey, J. Allan, Jr.
Hovey, Graham
Howard, John B.

Howard, John R.
Howell, John I.
Hoyt, Mont P.
Hudson, Manley O., Jr.
Huebner, Lee W.
Huffington, Roy M.
Hughes, John
Hughes, Thomas L.
Huglin, Henry C.
Huizenga, John W.
Hummel, Arthur W., Jr.
Hunsberger, Warren S.
Hunter, Robert E.
Hunter-Gault, Charleyne
Huntington, Samuiel P.
Hurewitz, J. C.
Hurlock, James B.
Huyck, Philip M.
Hyde, Henry B.
Hyde, James N.
Hyuland, Wiliam G.

I

Ikle, Fred C.
Ilchman, Alice S.
Inderfurth, Karl F.
Ingersol, Robert S.
Inman, B. R.
Ireland, R. L., III
Irwin, John N., II
Irwin, Wallace, Jr.
Isaacs, Norman E.
Isaacson, Walter
Iselin, John Jay
Issawi, Charles
Istel, Yves-Andre
Izlar, William H., Jr.

J

Jablonski, Wanda
Jacklin, Nancy P.
Jackson Elmore
Jackson, Eugene D.
Jackson, Henry F.
Jackson, John H.
Jackson, William E.
Jacobs, Eli S.

Jacobs, Norman
Jacobson, Harold K.
Jacobson, Jerome
Jaffe, Sam A.
James, John V.
Jamieson, J. K.
Janis, Mark W.
Janklow, Morton L.
Jansen, Marius B.
Jastrow, Robert
Javits, Jacob K.
Jaworski, Leon
Jervis, Robert L.
Jessup, Alpheus W.
Jessup, Philip C., Jr.
Johnson, Chalmers
Johnson, Harold K.
Johnson Howard W.
Johnson, Joseph E.
Johnson, L. Oakley
Johnson, Robbin S.
Johnson, W. Thomas, Jr.
Johnson, Willard R.
Johnstone, W. H.
Jones, David C.
Jones, Peter T.
Jones, Thomas V.
Jordan, Amos A.
Jordan, Vernon E., Jr.
Jorden,m William J.
Joseph, James A.
Josephson, William
Jungers, Frank
Junz, Helen B.

K

Kahan, Jerome H.
Kahin, George McT.
Kahler, Miles
Kahn, Harry
Kahn Herman
Kaiser, Philip M.
Kaiser, Robert G.
Kaiser, Walter J.
Kalb, Marvin
Kalicki, Jan
Kamarck, Andrew M.
Kaminer, Peter H.

Kamsky, Virginia Ann
Kaplan, Gilbert E.
Kaplan, Harold J.
Kaplan, Mark N.
Karalekas, Anne
Karnow, Stanley
Kassof, Allen H.
Katz, Milton
Katzenback, Nicholas deB.
Katzenstein, Peter J.
Kaufman, Henry
Kaufmann, William W.
Kaysen, Carl
Kearley, Anne
Keenan, Edward L.
Keeny, Spurgeon M., Jr.
Kelleher, Catherine M.
Kellen, Stephen M.
Keller, George M.
Kelly, George Armstrong
Kemp, Geoffrey
Kempner, Maximilian W.
Kenen, Peter B.
Keniston, Kenneth
Kennan, Elizabeth T.
Kennan, George T.
Kennedy, David M.
Kenney, F. Donald
Koehane, Nannerl O.
Keohane, Robert O.
Keppel, Francis
Kern, Harry F.
Kester, John G.
Ketelsen, James L.
Keydel, John F.
Khuri, Nicola N.
Kieschnick, W. F.
Kilpatrick, Robert D.
Kimmitt, Robert M.
King, James E.
King, John A., Jr.
Kintner, William R.
Kirk, Grayson
Kirkland, Lane
Kirkpatrick, Jeane J.
Kissinger, Henry A.
Kitchen, Jeffrey C.
Klaerner, Curtis M.
Kleiman, Robert

Klein, David
Klein, Edward
Klotz, Frank G.
Knight, Robert Huntington
Knoppers, Antonie T.
Knowlton, William A.
Knowlton, Winthrop
Kohler, Foy D.
Kolodziej, Edward A.
Komer, Robert W.
Koonce, Wayne A.
Koppel, Ted
Korb, Lawrence J.
Korbonski, Andrzej
Korry, Edward M.
Kraar, Louis
Kraemer, Lillian E.
Kraft, Joseph
Kramer, Jane
Krause, Lawrence B.
Kreczko, Alan J.
Kreidler, Robert N.
Kreisberg, Paul H.
Kreps, Juanita M.
Krisher, Bernard
Kristol, Irving
Kruidenier, David
Kubisch, Jack B.
Kurth, James R.

L

Labbock, Miriam H.
Labouisse, Henry R.
Lacy, Alex S.
Lacy, Dan M.
Lake, W. Anthony
Lall, Betty Goetz
Lambrinides, Andrea H.
Lamm. Donald S.
Lamontagne, Raymond A.
Lamson, Roy, Jr.
Landry, Lionel
Langer, Paul F.
Lansner, Kermit
LaPalombara, Joseph
Lapham, Lewis H.
Lary, Hal B.
Lauinger, Philip C., Jr.

Laukhuff, Perry
Laurenson, Edwin C.
Laventhol, David A.
Lazarus, Ralph
Lazarus, Steven
LeBaron, Eugene
LeBlond, Richard K., II
Leddy, John M.
Lederberg, Joshua
Lederer, Ivo John
Lee, Ernest S.
Lee, James E.
Lee, John M.
Lee, William L.
Leebaert, Derek
Lefever, Ernest W.
Leghorn, Richard S.
Legvold, Robert H.
Lehman, John R.
Lehman, Orin
Lehrer, Jim
Lehrman, Hal
Leich, John Foster
Leigh, Monroe
Leland, Marc E.
LeMelle, Tilden J.
LeMelle, Wilbert J.
Lemnitzer, Lyman L.
LeMoyne, James G.
Leonard, James F.
Leonard, James G.
Leslie, John E.
Le Sueur, Lawrence E.
Levine, Irving R.
Levitas, Mitchel
Levy, Marion J., Jr.
Levy, Walter J.
Lewis, Bernard
Lewis, Flora
Lewis, John P.
Lewis, John Wilson
Lewis, Samuel W.
Li, Vistor H.
Lichtblau, John H.
Lieberman, Henry R.
Lieberthal, Kenneth
Liffers, William A.
Lindquist, Warren T.
Lindsay, Franklin A.

170

Lindsay, George N.
Lindsay, John V.
Linen, James A.
Linowitz, Sol M.
Lipper, Kenneth
Lipscomb, James S.
Lipscomb, Thomas H.
Lipset, Seymour Martin
Lipson, Leon
Lissakers, Karin M.
Little, David
Livingston, Robert Gerald
Locke, Edwin A., Jr.
Lockwood, John E.
Lodal, Jan M.
Lodge, George C.
Loeb, Frances Lehman
Loeb, John L.
Loeb, Marshall
Loft, George
Long, Franklin A.
Loomis, Henry
Loos, A. Wiliam
Lord, Charles Edwin
Lord, Winston
Love, Ben F.
Lovelace, Jon B., Jr.
Lovestone, Jay
Low, Stephen
Lowe, Eugene Y., Jr.
Lowenfeld, Andreas F.
Lowenstein, James G.
Lowenthal, Abraham F.
Loy, Frank E.
Lubar, Robert A.
Lubman, Stanley B.
Luce, Charles F.
Luck, Edward C.
Luckey, E. Hugh
Ludt, Rudolph E.
Luers, William H.
Luke, David L. III
Lupfer, Timothy T.
Lustick, Ian S.
Luter, Yvonne
Luttwak, Edward N.
Lyet, J. Paul
Lyford, Joseph P.
Lyman, Richard W.

Lynch, Edward S.
Lynn, James T.
Lyn, Laurence E., Jr.
Lyon, E. Wilson
Lyion, Roger A.
Lythcott, George I.

M

McCarthy, John G.
McCarthy, Robert E.
McCloy, John J.
McCloy, John J., II
McColough, C. Peter
McCormack, Elizabeth J.
McCormick, Brooks
McCracken, Paul W.
McDonald, Alonzo L.
McDonald, Randal B.
McDonough, William J.
McDougal, Myres S.
McGee, Dale W.
McGhee, George C.
McGiffert, David E.
McGovern, Geroge S.
McHenry, Donald F.
McKee, James W., Jr.
McKeever, Porter
McKinley, John K.
McKiney, Robert M.
McLean, Sheila Avrin
McLin, Jon B.
McNamara, Robert S.
McNeill, Robert L.
McPherson, Harry C., Jr.
McQuade, Lawrence C.
MacArthur, Douglas, II
MacCormack, Charles F.
MacDonald, Gordon J.
MacEachron, David W.
MacGregor, Ian K.
MacLaury, Bruce K.
Machlup, Fritz
Machold, William F.
Macomber, John D.
Macomber, William B.
Macy, Robert M., Jr.
Maged, Mark J.
Magowan, Peter A.

Mahoney, Margaret E.
Mahoney, Thomas H., IV
Maier, Charles S.
Malin, Clement B.
Mallery, Richard
Malmgren, Harald B.
Manca, Marie Antoinette
Mangels, John D.
Manilow, Lewis
Manning, Bayless
Manning, Robert J.
Mansager, Felix, N.
Manshel, Warren Demian
Marcy, Carl
Marder, Murrey
Mark, David E.
Marks, Andrew H.
Marks, Leonard H.
Marks, Russel E., Jr.
Marmor, Theodore R.
Marous, John C.
Marron, Donald B.
Marshak, Robert E.
Marshall, C. Burton
Martin, David A.
Martin, Edwin M.
Martin, Malcolm W.
Martin, William McC., Jr.
Martinuzzi, Leo S., Jr.
Mason, Elvis L.
Masten, John E.
Mathews, Michael S.
Mathias, Charles McC., Jr.
Matteson, William B.
Maw, Carlyle E.
May, Clifford D.
May, Ernest R.
Mayer, Gerald M., Jr.
Mayer, Lawrence A.
Maynard, Robet C.
Maynes, Charles William
Mead, Dana G.
Meadows, Dennis L.
Meagher, Robert F.
Mehta, Ved
Meister, Irene W.
Melville, Richard A.
Mendlovitz, Saul H.
Menke, John R.

Merow, John E.
Merritt, Jafck N.
Meselson, Matthew
Messner, William C., Jr.
Metcalf, George R.
Mettler, Ruben R.
Meyer, Albert J.
Meyer, Charles A.
Meyer, Cord, Jr.
Meyer, Edward C.
Meyer, John R.
Meyer, Karl E.
Meyerson, Adam
Meyerson, Martin
Mickelson, Sig
Middleton, Drew
Midgley, Elizabeth
Millard, Mark J.
Miller, Charles D.
Miller, Franklin C.
Miller, Frederic A.
Miller, G. William
Miller, J. Irwin
Miller, Joyce D.
Miller Judith A.
Miller, Paul L.
Miller, William G.
Miller, William J.
Mills, Bradford
Mladek, Jan V.
Modomi, Fern Gold
Moe, Sherwood G.
Moller, John V., Jr.
Mondale, Walter F.
Monson, Judith H.
Montgomery, Park G.
Moody, William S.
Moore, John Norton
Moore, Jonathan
Moore, Maurice T.
Moore, Paul, Jr.
Moose, Richard M.
Morgan, Cecil
Morgan, Lee L.
Morgan, Thomas E.
Morgenthau, Lucinda L. Franks
Morley, James William
Morrell, Gene P.
Morris Grinnell

Morris, Max K.
Morrisett, Lloyd N.
Morse, David A.
Morse, Edward L.
Morse, F. Bradford
Morse, Kenneth P.
Moses, Alfred H.
Moyers, Bill D.
Moynihan, Daniel P.
Mujal-Leon, Eusebio M.
Mulford, David C.
Mulholland, William D.
Muller, Steven
Munger, Edwin S.
Munroe, George B.
Munroe, Vernon, Jr.
Munyan, Winthrop R.
Murphy, Grayson M-P.
Murray, Allen E.
Murray, Douglas P.
Muse, Martha Twitchell
Muskie, Edmund S.
Myerson, Bess

N

Nachmanoff, Arnold
Nacht, Michael L.
Nagorski, Zygmunt, Jr.
Nason, John W.
Nathan, James A.
Nathan, Robert R.
Nau, Henry R.
Neal, Alfred C.
Negroponte, John D.
Nelson, Clifford C.
Nelson, Merlin E.
Neustadt, Richard E.
Newburg, Andre W. G.
Newell, Barbara W.
Newhouse, John
Newman, Richard T.
Newsom, David D.
Newton, Quigg, Jr.
Ney, Edward N.
Nichols, Rodney W.
Niehuss, John M.
Nielsen, Waldermar A.
Nierenberg, William A.

Nimetz, Matthew
Nitze, Paul H.
Nolte, Richard H.
Nooter, Robert H.
Norman, William S.
Norstad, Lauris
Norton, Eleanor Holmes
Nossiter, Bernard D.
Notestein, Frank W.
Novak, Michael
Noyes, Charles Phelps
Nye, Joseph S.

O

Oakes, John B.
Oberdorfer, Don
Ochmanek, David A.
Odeen, Philip A.
Odom, William E.
O'Donnell, John
O'Donnell, Kevin
Oettinger, Anthony G.
Offit, Morris W.
O'Flaherty, J. Daniel
Ogden, Alfred
Ogden, William S.
O'Keefe, Bernard J.
Okimoto, Daniel I.
Oksenberg, Michel
Oliver, Covey T.
Olmstead, Cecil J.
Olsen, Leif H.
Olson, Lawrence
Olson, William C.
Olvey, Lee D.
O'Malley, Cormac K. H.
O'Neill, Michael J.
Opel, John R.
Oppenheimer, Franz M.
Ornstein, Norman J.
Obsorn, George K.
Osborne, Richard de J.
Osgood, Robert E.
Osmer, Margaret
Osnos, Peter
Ostrander, F. Taylor, Jr.
Overby, Andrew N.
Owen, Henry

Owen, Roberts B.
Oxman, Stephen A.
Oxnam, Robert B.

P

Packard, George R.
Paffrath, Leslie
Page, Howard W.
Page, John H.
Page, Walter H.
Pais, Abraham
Paley, William S.
Palm, Gregory K.
Palmer, Norman D.
Palmer, Ronald D.
Palmieri, Victor H.
Panofsky, Wolfgang K.H.
Parker, Daniel
Parker, Maynard
Parsky, Gerald L.
Passin, Herbert
Patrick, Hugh T.
Patterson, Charles J.
Patterson, Ellmore C.
Patterson, Gardner
Patterson, Hugh B., Jr.
Patterson, Robert P., Jr.
Pauker, Guy, J.
Paul, Roland A.
Payne, Samuel B.
Pearce, William R.
Pearson, John E.
Peay, T. Michael
Pedersen, Richard F.
Pelgrift, Kathryn C.
Pell, Claiborne
Penfield, James K.
Pennoyer, Robert M.
Peretz, Don
Perkins, James A.
Perkins, Roswell B.
Perle, Richard N.
Perlmutter, Amos
Perry, Hart
Peters, Arthur King
Petersen, Donald E.
Petersen, Gustav H.
Petersen, Howard C.

Petersen, S. R.
Peterson, Peter G.
Peterson, Rudolph A.
Petree, Richard W.
Petree, Richard W., Jr.
Petschek, Stephen R.
Petty, John R.
Pfaltzgraff, Robert L.
Pfeiffer, Jane Cahill
Pfeiffer, Ralph A., Jr.
Phillips, Christopher H.
Phillips, John G.
Phillips, Russell A., Jr.
Phleger, Herman
Pickens, T. Boone, Jr.
Picker, Harvey
Picker, Jean
Pickering, Thomas R.
Piel, Gerard
Pierce, Kerry K.
Pierce, William C.
Piercy, George T.
Pierotti, Roland
Pierre, Andrew J.
Pifer, Alan
Pigott, Charles M.
Pilliod, Charles J., Jr.
Pincus, Lionel I.
Pincus, Walter H.
Pino, John A.
Pinola, Joseph J.
Pipes, Daniel
Pipes, Richard E.
Pippitt, Robert M.
Place, John B. M.
Plank, John N.
Platig, E. Raymond
Platt, Jonas M.
Platt, Nicholas
Platten, Donald C.
Plimpton, Calvin H.
Plimpton, Francis T. P.
Podhoretz, Norman
Polk, William R.
Pollack, Gerald A.
Polsby, Nelson
Pool, Ithiel DeSola
Poor, J. Sheppard
Portes, Richard D.

Posner, Michael H.
Posvar, Wesley W.
Potter, Robert S.
Power, Philip H.
Power, Sarah Goddard
Power, Thomas F., Jr.
Powers, Joshua B.
Powers, Thomas Moore
Pranger, Robert J.
Pratt, Edmund T., Jr.
Press, Frank
Preston, Lewis T.
Prewitt, Kenneth
Price, John R., Jr.
Price, Robert
Puckett, Allen E.
Pugh, Richard C.
Pulitzer, Michael E.
Pulling, Edward
Purcell, Susan Kaufman
Pursley, Robert E.
Pursey, Nathan M.
Pustay, John S.
Putignano, Patrick A.
Putnam, George E., Jr.
Putnam, Robert D.
Pye, Lucian W.

Q

Quandt, William B.
Quester, George H.
Quigg, Philip W.
Quigley, Leonard V.

R

Rabb, Maxwell M.
Rabi, Isidor I.
Rabinowitch, Victor
Radway, Laurence I.
Ramsey, Douglas K.
Randolph, R. Sean
Ranis, Gustav
Rashish, Myer
Rather, Dan
Rathjens, George W.
Rattner, Steven L.
Rauch, Rudolph S., III

173

Ravenal, Earl C.
Ravenholt, Albert
Rawson, Merle R.
Raymond, David A.
Raymond, Jack
Read, Benjamin H.
Reed, J. V., Jr.
Reed, Philip D.
Reeves, Jay B. L.
Regan, John M., Jr.
Rehm, John B.
Reid, Ogden, R.
Reid, Whitelaw
Reinhardt, John E.
Reisman, Michael M.
Renfrew, Charles B.
Resor, Stanley R.
Reston, James B.
Revelle, Roger
Rey, Nicholas A.
Reynold, Lloyd G.
Rhinelander, John B.
Rhinesmith, Stephen H.
Rhodes, John B., Jr.
Ribicoff, Abraham A.
Rice, Emmett J.
Rich, John H., Jr.
Richard, Eric L.
Richardson, David B.
Richardson, Elliot L.
Richardson, John, Jr.
Richardson, Richard W.
Richardson, William R.
Ridgway, Roxanne L.
Rielly, John E.
Ries, Hans A.
Riesel, Victor
Ripley, S. Dillon, II
Rivers, Richard R.
Rivkin, Donald H.
Rivlin, Alice M.
Robbins, Donald G., Jr.
Roberts, Chalmers M.
Robets, Walter Orr
Robinson, Charles W.
Robinson, James D., III
Robinson, Marshall A.
Robinson, Michael D.
Robinson, Randall

Robison, Olin C.
Roche, John P.
Rockefeller, David
Rockefeller, John D., IV
Rockefeller, Rodman C.
Rodman, Peter W.
Rodriguez, Vincent A.
Roett, Riordan
Roff, J. Hugh
Rogers, David E.
Rogers, David E.
Rogers, Nat S.
Rogers, William D.
Rogers, William P.
Rohlen Thomas P.
Roosa, Robet V.
Roosa, Ruth AmEnde
Roosevelt, Kermit
Root, Oren
Rose, Daniel
Rose, Elihu
Rose, Frederick P.
Rosecrance, Richard
Rosen, Jane K.
Rosenblum, Mort
Rosenfeld, Stephen S.
Rosengarten, Adolph G., Jr.
Rosenthal, A. M.
Rosenthal, Jack
Rosenwald, William
Rosin, Axel G.
Rosovksy, Henry
Ross, Roger
Rosso, David J.
Rostow, Eugene V.
Rostow, Walt W.
Rotberg, Robert I.
Roth, Richard H.
Roth, William M.
Roth, William V., Jr.
Rouse, James W.
Rowen, Henry S.
Rowny, Edward L.
Rubin, Robert M.
Rubin, Seymour J.
Ruckelshaus, William D.
Ruebhausen, Oscar M.
Ruenitz, Robert M.
Ruina, J. P.

Rush, Barney
Rush, Kenneth
Rusk, Dean
Russell, Harvey C.
Russell, T. W., Jr.
Rustow, Dankwart A.
Ruthberg, Miles N.
Ruttan, Vernon W.
Ryan, Hewson A.
Ryan, John T., Jr.
Ryan, John T. III

S

Sachs, Jeffrey D.
Safran, Nadav
Sage, Mildred D.
Said, Edward
Salisbury, Harrison E.
Salomon, Richard E.
Salomon, William R.
Saltzman, Chyarles E.
Salzman, Herbert
Sample, Steven B.
Samuel, Howard D.
Samuels, Michael A.
Samuels, Nathaniel
Sanford, Terry
Sargeant, Howland H.
Saul, Ralph S.
Saunders, Harold H.
Savage, Frank
Sawhill, John C.
Sawyer, Diane
Sawyer, John E.
Sawyier, Stephen K.
Scalapino, Robert A.
Scali, John A.
Schacht, Henry B.
Schachter, Oscar
Schaetzel, J. Robert
Schafer, John H.
Schallert, Edwin G.
Schaufele, William E., Jr.
Schecter, Jerold
Scheinman, Lawrence
Schell, Orville H., Jr.
Schiff, Frank W.
Schiff, John M.

Schilling, Warner R.
Schlesinger, Arthur, Jr.
Schlosser, Herbert S.
Schmertz, Herbert
Schmoker, John B.
Schneider, Jan
Schneier, Arthur
Schoettle, Enid C. B.
Schorr, Daniel L.
Schubert, Richard F.
Schuyler, C. V. R.
Schwab, Susan C.
Schwab, William B.
Schwartz, Harry
Schwarz, H. Marshall
Schwebel, Stephen M.
Scott, Harold B.
Scott, Stuart N.
Scoville, Herbert, Jr.
Scowcroft, Brent
Scranton, William W.
Scrimshaw, Nevin S.
Seaborg, Glenn T.
Seabury, Paul
Seagrave, Norman P.
Seamans, Robet C., Jr.
Segal, Sheldon J.
Segal, Susan L.
Seibold, Frederick C., Jr.
Seidman, Herta Lande
Seigenthaler, John L.
Seigle, John W.
Seitz, Frederick
Selin, Ivan
Sellers, Robert V.
Semple, Robert B., Jr.
Sewell, John W.
Sexton, William C.
Seymour, Whitney North
Shalala, Donna E.
Shapiro, Eli
Shapiro, George M.
Shapiro, Isaac
Shaplen Robert
Sharp, Daniel A.
Shayne, Herbert M.
Shearer, Warren W.
Sheeline, Paul C.
Sheffield, James R.

Sheinkman, Jack
Sheldon, Eleanor Bernert
Shelley, Sally Swing
Shelp, Ronald K.
Shelton, Sally A.
Shepherd, Mar, Jr.
Sherry, George L.
Sherwood, Richard E.
Shipley, Walter V.
Shirer, William L.
Shishkin, Boris
Shoemaker, Don
Shriver, R. Sargent, Jr.
Shulman, Colette
Shulman, Marshall D.
Shultz, George P.
Shute, Benjamin R.
Sick, Gary G.
Sigmund, Paul E.
Silberman, Laurence H.
Silk, Leonard S.
Silvers, Roibert B.
Simes, Dimitri K.
Sisco, Joseph J.
Skidmore, Thomas E.
Skinner, David E.
Skinner, Elliott P.
Skolnikoff, Eugene B.
Slater, Joseph E.
Slawson, John
Sloane, Anne B.
Slocombe, Walter B.
Slocum, John J.
Smart, S. Bruce, Jr.
Smith, Carleton Sprague
Smith, Datus, C., Jr.
Smith, David S.
Smith, DeWitt C., Jr.
Smith, Gaddis
Smith, Gerald C.
Smith, Hedrick L.
Smith, John T., II
Smith, Larry K.
Smith, Perry M.
Smith, Theodore M.
Smith, W. Mason
Smith, W. Y.
Smyth, Henry DeW.
Smythe, Mabel M.

Sneath, William S.
Sneider, Richard L.
Sohn, Louis B.
Solarz, Stephen J.
Solbert, Peter O. A.
Solomon, Adam
Solomon, Anthony M.
Solomon, Richard H.
Solomon, Robert
Sonne, Christian R.
Sonnenfeldt, Helmut
Sonnenfeldt, Richard W.
Sorensen, Gillian Martin
Sorensen, Theodore C.
Soubry, Emile E.
Southard, Frank A., Jr.
Sovern, Michael I.
Spain, James W.
Spang, Kenneth M.
Spector, Phillip L.
Spencer, Edson W.
Spencer, John H.
Spencer, William C.
Spero, Joan E.
Spiegel, Marianne A.
Sppiers, Ronald I.
Spiro, Herbert J.
Spofford, Charles M.
Sprague, Robert C.
Squadron, Howard M.
Stackpolie, Stephen H.
Staley, Eguene
Stalson, Helena
Stamas, Stephen
Stanley, Timothy W.
Stanton, Frank
Stanton, R. John, Jr.
Staples, Eugene S.
Starr, S. Frederick
Stassen, Harold E.
Stauffacher, Charles B.
Steadman, Richard C.
Stebbins, James H.
Steel, Ronald
Stein, Eric
Stein Howard
Steinbruner, John D.
Steiner, Daniel
Stent, Madelon Delany

Stepan, Alfred C.
Stern, Ernest
Stern, Fritz
Stern, H. Peter
Sternlight, David
Stevens, Charles R.
Stevens, James W.
Stevens, Norton
Stevenson, Adlai E., III
Stevenson, H. L.
Stevenson, John R.
Stewart, Donald M.
Stewart, Patricia Carry
Stewart, Ruth Ann
Sticht, J. Paul
Stifel, Laurence D.
Stilwell, Richrd G.
Stobaugh, Robert B.
Stoessel, Walter J., Jr.
Stoessinger, John G.
Stoga, Alan
Stone, Jeremy J.
Stone, Robert G., Jr.
Stone, Roger D.
Stone, Shepard
Stookey, John Hoyt
Stratton, Julius A.
Straus, Donald B.
Straus, Jack I.
Straus, Oscar S.
Straus, R. Peter
Straus, Ralph I.
Straus, Robert K.
Strauss, Robert S.
Strauss, Simon D.
Strausz-Hupe, Robert
Strayer, Joseph R.
Stremlau, John J.
Stroud, Joe H.
Sullivan, Eugene J.
Sullivan, William H.
Sunderland, Jack B.
Surrey, Walter Sterling
Suslow, Low A.
Sutterlin, James S.
Sutton, Francis X.
Swank, Emory C.
Swanson, David H.
Swearer, Howard R.

Sweitzer, Brandon W.
Swenson, Eric P.
Swing, John Temple
Swinton, Stanley M.
Symington, W. Stuart
Szanton, Peter L.

T

Taber, George M.
Talbot, Phillips
Talbott, Strobe
Tanham, George K.
Tannenwald, Theodore, Jr.
Tanner, Harold
Tanter, Raymond
Taubman, William
Tavoulareas, William P.
Taylor, Arthur R.
Taylor, George E.
Taylor, Maxwell D.
Taylor, William J., Jr.
Teicher, Howard J.
Teitelbaum, Michael S.
Tempelsman, Maurice
Tennyson, Leonard B.
Thayer, Robert H.
Theobald, Thomas C.
Thoman, G. Richard
Thomas, Barbara S.
Thomas, Evan
Thomas Franklin
Thomas, Lee B., Jr.
Thomas, Lewis
Thompson, Edward T.
Thompson, W. Scott
Thompson, William Pratt
Thomson, James C., Jr.
Thornell, Richard P.
Thornton, Thomas P.
Thorp, Willard L.
Tillinghast, David R.
Tillman, Seth P.
Todaro, Michael P.
Todman, Terence A., Jr.
Tomlinson, Alexander C.
Topping, Seymour
Townsend, Edward
Trager, Frank N.

Train, Harry D., II
Train, Russell E.
Trani, Eugene P.
Travis, Martin B., Jr.
Tree, Marietta
Trees, James F.
Trewhitt, Henry L.
Trezise, Philip H.
Triffin, Robert
Troia, Kathleen
Trooboff, Peter D.
Trost, Carlisle A. H.
Trowbridge, Alexander B.
Tucher, H. Anton
Tuchman, Barbara
Tuck, Edward Hallam
Tucker, Robert W.
Tully, Darrow
Turkevich, John
Turner, Stansfield
Turner, William C.
Tuthill, Hohn W.
Tweedy, Gordon B.
Tyrrell, R. Emmett, Jr.

U

Udovitch, Abraham L.
Ullman, Richard H.
Ulman, Cornelius M.
Ulmer, Alfred C.
Ungar, Sanford J.
Unger, Leonard
Urfer, Richard P.
Usher, William R.
Utley, Garrick
Uzielli, Giorgio

V

Vagliano, Alexander M.
Vaky, Viron P.
Valdez, Abelardo Lopez
Vance, Cyrus R.
van den Haag, Ernest
Van Slyck, DeForest
Van Vlierden, Constant M.
Veit, Lawrence A.
Veliotes, Nicholas A.

Vermilye, Peter H.
Vernon, Raymond
Vershbow, Alexander R.
Vessey, John W., Jr.
Vogelgesang, Sandy
Vojta, George J.
Volcker, Paul A.
Von Klemperer, Alfred H.
Von Mehren, Robert B.

W

Wadsworth, Mary Ames
Wagley, Charles W.
Wahl, Nicholas
Waidelich, Charles J.
Walinsky, Adam
Walker, A. Lightfoot
Walker, Charls E.
Walker, G. R.
Walker, George G.
Walker, Joseph, Jr.
Walker, William N.
Walkowicz, T. F.
Wallace, Martha R.
Wallich, Henry C.
Wallis, Gordon T.
Walters, Barbara
Waltz, Kenneth N.
Ward, F. Champion
Ward, Martin J.
Warner, Edward L., III
Warner, Rawleigh, Jr.
Warnke, Paul C.
Washburn, Abbott M.
Waters, James F., Jr.
Watson, Craig M.
Watson, Thomas J., Jr.
Watts, Glenn E.
Watts, John H., III
Watts, William
Way, Alva O.
Weaver, George L.-P.
Webster, Bethuel M.
Wehrle, Leroy S.
Weidenbaum, Murray L.
Weiksner, George B., Jr.
Weil, Frank A.
Weinberger, Caspar W.

Weiner, Myron
Weiss, Edith Brown
Welch, Jasper A., Jr.
Weller, Ralph A.
Wells, Herman B.
Wells, Louis T., Jr.
Wender, Ira T.
Wetheim, Mitzi M.
Wesely, Edwin J.
Wessell, Nils Y.
West, J. Robinson
West, Robert LeRoy
Westphal, Albert C. F.
Wexler, Anne
Whalen, Charles W., Jr.
Wharton, Clifton R., Jr.
Wheat, Francis M.
Wheeler, John K.
Wheeler, John P. III
Wheeler, Richard W.
Whipple, Taggart
Whitaker, Jennifer Seymore
Whitaker, Mark
White, Barbara M.
White, Betsy Buttrill
White, Frank X.
White, Robert J.
White, Theodore H.
Whitehead, John C.
Whitehouse, Charles S.
Whiting, Allen S.
Whitman, Marina v. N.
Whitney, Craig R.
Whitridge, Arnold
Wickham, John A., Jr.
Wiesner, Jerome B.
Wilbur, Brayton, Jr.
Wilcox, Francis O.
Wilcox, Robert B.
Willdavsky, Aaron
Wilds, Walter W.
Wiley, Richard A.
Wiley, W. Bradford
Wilhelm, Harry E.
Wilkins, Roger W.
Will, George F.
Willes, Mark H.
Willey, Fay
Williams, Franklin Hall

Williams, Harold M.
Williams, Haydn
Williams, Janes B.
Williams, Joseph H.
Williams, Maurice J.
Willrich, Mason
Wilson, Carroll L.
Wilson, Donal M.
Wilson, James Q.
Wilson, John D.
Wimpfheimer, Jacques D.
Winder, R. Bayly
Windmuller, Thomas S.
Wingate, Henry S.
Winks, Robin W.
Winslow, Richard S.
Winterer, Philip S.
Wisner, Frank G., II
Witunski, Michael
Wofford, Harris L.
Wohlstetter, Albert
Wohlstetter, Roberta
Wolf, Charles, Jr.
Wolf, Milton A.
Wolfensohn, James D.
Wolff, Alan Wm.
Wolfowitz, Paul D.
Wood, Harleston R.
Wood, Richard D.
Woodside, Wiliam S.
Woolf, Harry
Woolsey, R. James
Wriggins, W. Howard
Wright, Jerauld
Wriston, Walter B.
Wyle, Frederick S.
Wyman, Thomas H.

Y

Yang, Chen Ning
Yankelovich, Daniel
Yarmolinsky, Adam
Yeo, Edwin H., III
Yergin, Daniel H.
Yntema, Theodore O.
Yoder, Edwin M., Jr.
Young, Alice
Young, Andrew

Young, Edgar B.
Young, Richard
Young, Stephen B.
Youngman, William S.
Yu, Frederick T. C.
Yudkin, Richard A.

Z

Zagoria, Donald S.
Zarb, Frank G.
Zartman, I. William
Zeidenstein, George
Zelnick, C. Robert
Zilkha, Ezra K.
Zimmerman, Edwin M.
Zimmerman, William
Zimmermann, Warren
Zinberg, Dorothy S.
Zorthian, Barry
Zraket, Charles A.
Zumwalt, E. R., Jr.

Appendix III

THE TRILATERAL COMMISSION
As of October 15, 1982

David Rockefeller, *North American
Chairman*
Mitchell Sharp, *North American Deputy
Chairman*
Charles B. Heck, *North American Director*
Georges Berthoin, *European Chairman*
Egidio Ortona, *European Deputy Chairman*
Paul Revay, *European Director*
Takeshi Watanabe, *Japanese Chairman*
Nobuhiko Ushiba, *Japanese Deputy
Chairman*
Tadashi Yamamoto, *Japanese Director*

North American Members
David M. Abshire, *Chairman, Georgetown
University Center for Strategic and
International Studies; former U.S. Assistant
Secretary of State for Congressional Relations.*
Gardner Ackley, *Henry Carter Adams
University Professor of Political Economy,
University of Michigan; former Member,
U.S. Council of Economic Advisors*
Graham Allison, *Dean, John F. Kennedy
School of Government; Harvard University*
Robert Andras, O.C., *Senior Vice President,
Tech Corporation; former Member of Canadian
Parliament*
Bruce Babbitt, *Governor of Arizona*
Michel Belanger, *President and Chief
Executive Officer, National Bank of Canada*
Lucy Wilson Benson, *Corporate Director and
Consultant to Business and Government; former
U.S. Under Secretary of State for Security
Assistance, Science and Technology*
Conrad M. Black, *Chairman, Argus
Corporation, Ltd., Toronto; Chairman, Norcen
Energy Resources, Ltd.*
Robert R. Bowie, *Guest Scholar, The
Brookings Institution; former Deputy Director,
Central Intelligence Agency*
John Brademas, *President, New York
University; former Member of U.S. House of*

Representatives
Herb Breau, *Member of Canadian Parliament*
Andrew F. Brimmer, *President, Brimmer &
Company, Inc.; former Member of Board of
Governors, U.S. Federal Reserve System*
Harold Brown, *Distinguished Visiting
Professor of National Security Affairs, Johns
Hopkins University School of Advanced
International Studies; former U.S. Secretary
of Defense*
*Zbigniew Brzezinski, *Senior Adviser, George-
town University Center for Strategic and
International Studies; former U.S. Assistant to
the President for National Security Affairs*
John F. Burlingame, *Vice Chairman of the
Board and Executive Officer, General Electric
Company*
George Busbee, *Governor of Georgia*
Philip Caldwell, *Chairman of the Board,
Ford Motor Company*
Hugh Calkins, *Partner, Jones, Day, Reavis
& Pogue.*
Claude Castonguay, *President and Chief
Executive Officer, The Laurentian Mutual
Assurance Company, Quebec, former Minister
in the Quebec Government*
Sol Chaikin, *President, International Ladies'
Garment Workers' Union*
Warren Christopher, *Senior Partner,
O'Melveny & Myers; former U.S. Deputy
Secretary of State*
William S. Cohen, *Member of U.S. Senate*
*William T. Coleman, Jr., *Senior Partner,
O'Melveny & Myers; former U.S. Secretary of
Transportation*
Barber B. Conable, Jr., *Member of U.S. House
of Representatives*
Gail C. A. Cook, *Executive Vice President,
Bennecon Ltd., Toronto*
Richard N. Cooper, *Maurits Boas Professor
of International Economics, Harvard
University; former U.S. Under Secretary*

Milbank, Tweed, Hadley and McCloy; *former U.S. Secretary of Defense;, Attorney General and Ambassador to Great Britain*
John E. Rielly, *President The Chicago Council on Foreign Relations*
*Charles W. Robinson, *Chairman, Energy Transition Corporation; former U.S. Deputy Secretary of State*
*David Rockefeller
John D. Rockefeller, IV, *Governor of West Virginia*
Robert V. Roosa, *Partner, Brown Brothers Harriman & Co.*
William V. Roth, Jr., *Member of U.S. Senate*
John C. Sawhill, *Director and Senior Partner, McKinsey & Company; former U.S. Deputy Secretary of Energy; former President, New York University*
J. Robert Schaetzel, *Former, U.S. Ambassador to the European Communities*
*Mitchell Sharp, *Commissioner, Northern Pipline Agency; former Canadian Secretary of State for External Affairs*
Mark Shepherd, Jr., *Chairman, Texas Instruments Incorporated*
Joseph J. Sisco, *Partner, Sisco Associates; former President, American University; former U.S. Under Secretary of State for Political Affairs*
Gerard C. Smith, *Former Head of U.S. Arms Control and Disarmament Agency and Chief Negotiator of SALT I; former Ambassador at Large for Non-Proliferation Matters*
Anthony M. Solomon, *President, Federal Reserve Bank of New York; former U.S. Under Secretary of the Treasury for Monetary Affairs*
Helmut Sonnenfeldt, *Guest Scholar, The Brookings Institution; former Counselor, U.S. State Department*
Robert S. Strauss, *Partner, Akin, Gump Strauss, Hauer &Feld; former U.S. Special Trade Representative*
Russell E. Train, *President, World Wildlife Fund-U.S.; former Administrator, U.S. Environmental Protection Agency*
Philip H. Trezise, *Senior Fellow, The Brookings Institution; former U.S. Assistant Secretary of State for Economic Affairs*
G.A. Van Wielingen, *Chairman and Chief Executive Officer, Sulpetro Limited, Calgary*

Martha R. Wallace, *Director, The Henry Luce Foundation, Inc.*
Haskell G. Ward, *President, Haskell G. Ward Associates; former Deputy Mayor of New York City*
Paul C. Warnke, *Partner, Clifford and Warnke; former Director, U.S. Arms Control and Disarmament Agency and Chief Negotiator of SALT II*
*J.H. Warren, *Vice Chairman, Bank of Montreal*
Glenn E. Watts, *President, Communications Workers of America*
George Weyerhaeuser, *President and Chief Executive Officer, Weyerhaeuser Company*
John C. Whitehead, *Senior Partner, Goldman, Sachs & Co.*
Marina V.N. Whitman, *Vice President and Chief Economist, General Motors Corporation; former Member, U.S. Council of Economic Advisors*
*T.A. Wilson, *Chairman of the Board, The Boeing Company*
Andrew Young, *Mayor of Atlanta; former U.S. Ambassador to the United Nations*

Former Members in Public Service
William Brock, *U.S. Special Trade Representative*
Arthur F. Burns, *U.S. Ambassador to the Federal Republic of Germany*
George Bush, *Vice President of the United States*
William A. Hewitt, *U.S. Ambassador to Jamaica*
Michael J.L. Kirby, *Canadian Secretary to the Cabinet for Federal-Provincial Relations*
Paul A. Volcker, *Chairman, Board of Governors, U.S. Federal Reserve System*
Caspar W. Weinberger, *U.S. Secretary of Defense*

Current and Former Major Financial Supporters in the United States (since the founding of The Trilateral Commission in 1973)
(As of March 31, 1980)

Foundations
William H. Donner Foundation, Inc.

BIBLIOGRAPHY

CONSPIRACY

Acton, Lord, *Cambridge Modern History: The French Revolution,* Volume VIII, New York, Macmillan, 1904.
Illuminati (suppressed in Bavaria in 1784, reportedly) leaders taught that all kings were unnecessary and were tools of despotism. Alois Hofmann, Professor of Rhetoric at Vienna and a friend of Emperor Leopold, traced (in his newspaper *Wiener Zeitung*) the renewed revolutionary agitation in Bavaria to the Illuminati and a universal conspiracy it had planned. He recommended that the Jesuits should be revived to combat it. An agent of the Directory reported renewed activity of the Illuminati in 1796. The French arrived with their revolutionary doctrines of Illuminism in Germany in 1880.

Eaton, Clement, *History of the Southern Confederacy,* New York, Macmillan, 1954.
Tells of Rothschild-connected Erlanger financing of the Confederacy.

Machiavelli, Niccolo, *The Prince,* Chicago, Encyclopedia Britannica, 1955.
The basic textbook for conspirators.

Manly, Chesly, *The Twenty Year Revolution,* Henry Regnery, Chicago, 1954.

Martin, Rose L., *The Fabian Freeway,* Boston and Los Angeles, Western Islands, 1966.
Best general review of activities of the *Insiders* in fields other than finance.

Marx, Karl, *The Communist Manifesto,* Gateway Edition reprinted by Henry Regnery Company, Chicago.
Marx' ten planks for communizing a country should be memorized by everyone.

Robinson, John, *Proofs of a Conspiracy,* reprinted by Western Islands, Boston & Los Angeles.
Revealing the history of the forces behind the French Revolution. First published in 1798.

Webster, Nesta, *Secret Societies and Subversive Movements,* reprinted by Christian Book Club, Hawthorne, Calif., 1967.
A basic text on the subject by a careful English historian.

Webster, Nesta, *The French Revolution,* reprinted by Christian Book Club, Hawthorne, Calif., 1969.
Role of Illuminati in the first Communist Revolution.

Webster, Nesta, and Gittens, Anthony, *World Revolution,* Britons, Devon, England, 1972.
This basic text has been brought up to date from its 1921 publication by Mr. Gittens, a member of Mrs. Webster's research team since the 1920's.

FEDERAL RESERVE

Allen, Frederick Lewis, "Morgan The Great," *Life,* April 25, 1949.
Provides information on Morgan's role in precipitating the Panic of 1907.

American Heritage, August 1965 (See *Financial Chronicle,* March 9, 1929).
Quotes Warburg's warning of impending disaster concerning the stock market.

Aydelotte, Frank, *The American Rhodes Scholarships,* Princeton University Press, 1946.
Includes information on Rhodes' motivation in setting up the scholarships.

Bryan, William "John," *The United States Unresolved Monetary and Political*

Problems. Privately published.

Corti, Count Egon, *The Rise of the House of Rothschild*, New York, Grosset & Dunlap, 1928.
Possibly the best balanced study of Rothschilds. Most books are either slavishly adulatory or tend to blame everything since the fall of Adam on the Rothschilds.

Dobbs, Zygmund, *Keynes At Harvard* (Revised and Enlarged Edition), W. Sayville, N. Y., Probe Research, Inc., 1969.
Economic Deception as a Political Credo; combines a layman's explanation of Keynesian economics and its effect with an excellent rundown on who promotes the system and why.

Groseclose, Elgin, *Fifty Years of Managed Money*, New York, Spartan, 1965.
What Keynesians, politicians, bureaucrats and the Federal Reserve have done to our money system.

Money and Man, New York, Frederick Ungal, 1967.
Excellent history of money.

Hansl, Proctor, *Years of Plunder*, New York, Smith & Haas, 1935.
Covers events leading up to the crash of 1929.

Hargrave, John, *Montagu Norman*, New York, Greystone Press, 1942.
Norman was a key *Insider* who traveled the world coodinating the moves of international finance.

Hinton, Harold Boaz, *Cordell Hull*, Garden City, N. Y., Doubleday Doran & Co., Inc., 1942.

House, "Colonel" Edward Mandel, *Philip Dru: Administrator: A Story of Tomorrow, 1920-1935*, New York, B. W. Huebsch, 1920.

Hull, Cordell, *Memoirs*, New York, Collier-Macmillan, 1948.
Reveals Hull's shock when Senator Nelson Aldrich introduced the progressive income tax in the Senate.

Keynes, John Maynard, *The General Theory of Employment, Interest and Money*, New York, Harcourt, Brace and Co., 1958.

Kolko, Gabriel, *The Triumph of Conservatism*, Chicago, Quadrangle Books, 1967.
Probably the best general refutation of the popularly held belief that the "Progressive Era" was instigated and run by representatives of the "downtrodden masses." This book is especially good on the establishment of the Federal Reserve System.

Lindbergh, Charles A. Sr., *The Economic Pinch*, Phil., Dorrance & Company, Inc., 1923.
Chronicles the Federal Reserve and international bankers' first whipsaw of the economy after the establishment of the Federal Reserve.

Lundberg, Ferdinand, *America's 60 Families*, New York, Vanguard, 1938.
Especially good on Wall Street control of Woodrow Wilson.

McAdoo, William G., *Crowded Years*, New York, Houghton-Mifflin, 1931.
Reveals cynicism of Wall Streeters in opposing the Federal Reserve Act.

Morton, Frederic, *The Rothschilds: A Family Portrait*. New York, Atheneum, 1962.
Although adulatory, this book contains many useful clues which, when pieced together with other information, fills in part of the puzzle.

Myers, Gustavus, *History of the Great American Fortunes*, New York, Random House, 1936.
Mentions the role of the European Rothschilds in American financial affairs.

184

Noyes, Alexander Dana, *The Market Place*, Boston, Little, Brown & Company, 1938.
Describes events leading up to the depression of 1929.

Pratt, Sereno S., *The Work of Wall Street*, New York, Appleton & Company, 1916.
Discloses the role of Wall Street in precipitating the 1929 stock market crash.

Primer On Money, A—Subcommittee on Domestic Finance, Committee on Banking and Currency, House of Representatives, 88th Congress, U. S. Govt. Printing Office, Washington, D. C.
Covers control of the Federal Reserve over money and banking.

Quigley, Carroll, *Tragedy and Hope*, New York, Macmillan, 1966.
Although Quigley is not opposed to the *Insiders*, his monumental opus discloses a century of machinations of the *Insiders* of international finance.

Rothbard, Murray, *America's Great Depression*, Los Angeles, Nash Publishing, 1972.
This is an excellent source for information on how the Federal Reserve brought on the great depression.

Rothbard, Murray, *What Has Government Done To Our Money?* Colorado Springs, Colo. Pine Tree Press.
Excellent pamphlet on the history of money and how it has been debauched.

Sennholz, Hans, "The Great Depression," *The Freeman*, October 1969.
Covers ways in which the government lengthened the depression.

Sparling, Earl, *Mystery Men of Wall Street*, New York, Greenberg, 1930.
Provides background on numerous Wilsonian era tycoons.

Vanderlip, Frank, "Farm Boy to Financier," *Saturday Evening Post*, February 9, 1935.
Extremely revealing article on the creation of the Federal Reserve by a man who played a key role in same.

Viereck, George S., *The Strangest Friendship in History*, New York, Liveright, 1932.
This very important book covers the role of "Colonel" House in the Woodrow Wilson Administration.

von Mises, Ludwig, *Human Action*, New Haven, Yale University Press, 1949.
The world's most profound advocate of free enterprise discusses why it works and why collectivism fails.

Voorhis, Jerry, *Out of Debt—Out of Danger*, New York, Devin-Adair, 1943.
The Congressman defeated by Richard Nixon at the start of Nixon's career in politics analyzes the consequences of the Federal Reserve-international bank control of the nation's money system.

Warburg, James, *The Long Road Home*, New York, Doubleday, 1964.
Mentions his father's role in creating the Federal Reserve.

Warburg, Paul, *The Federal Reserve System,* New York, Macmillan, 1930.
The story from the horse's mouth, but with many important deletions.

Wechsberg, Joseph, *The Merchant Bankers*, Boston, Little, Brown and Co., 1966.
Rundown on English *Insiders* including Rothschilds, Warburgs and Lehmans.

White, Andrew D., *Fiat Money Inflation in France*, Foundation for Economic Education, Irvington-on-Hudson, N. Y., 1959.
Describes the beginning of paper money flim-flams.

THE BOLSHEVIK REVOLUTION

Birmingham, Stephen, *Our Crowd*, New York, Dell, 1967.
Cites interesting background on Schiff and Warburg families.

Brasol, Boris, *The World At The Crossroads,* Boston, Hutchinson & Co., 1921.
Former Czarist official discusses Bolshevik Revolution and its financiers.

Budenz, Louis F., *Bolshevik Invasion of the West,* Linden, New Jersey, Bookmailer, 1966.
Notes the friendly relations between Wall Street and the Kremlin.

Creel, George, *The German-Bolshevik Conspiracy,* The Committee on Public Information, Wash., D. C., 1918.
Presents Sisson documents showing involvement of Max Warburg and other Germans in financing Lenin. Ignores New York financing of Trotsky.

de Goulevitch, Arsene, *Czarism and the Revolution,* [Reprinted by] Omni Publications, Hawthorne, Calif., 1961.
Quotes excellent account of the financing of the Bolsheviks.

Dillon, Dr. E. J., *The Inside Story of the Peace Conference,* New York, Harper & Brothers, 1920.
Most revealing on help given to Bolsheviks by *Insiders* at Versailles.

Forbes, B. O., *Men Who Are Making America,* New York, B. C. Forbes Publishing Company, Inc., 1922.
Contains biography of Schiff and covers his role in the establishment of the Federal Reserve and also his sympathy for the Bolsheviks.

Hagedorn, Herman, *The Magnate,* New York, John Day.
Refers to Morgan's front man being involved in the transfer of a million dollars to the Bolsheviks.

Hunter, Robert, *Revolution, Why, How, Where,* Harper & Brothers, New York, 1940.

Kennan, George F., *Russia And the West Under Lenin and Stalin,* Little, Brown & Co., 1960-61.

Kerensky, Alexander, *The Crucifixion of Liberty,* New York, John Day, 1934.
Quoted in Possony's *A Century of Conflict* as backing up the assertions of Edgar Sisson on the German-Bolshevik conspiracy.

Papers Relating to the Foreign Relations of the United States-Russia, 1918, House of Representatives Document No. 1868, Volume 1, U. S. Govt. Printing Office, Wash., D. C.
Covers the financing of the Bolshevik Revolution.

Seymour, Charles, *Intimate Papers of Colonel House,* New York, Houghton-Mifflin, 1928, 4 volumes.´
Very revealing in places when pieced together with other information.

Shub, David, *Lenin,* Baltimore, Md., Penguin Books, 1967.

Sisson, Edgar, *One Hundred Red Days: A Personal Chronicle of the Bolshevik Revolution,* New Haven, Yale, 1931.
Appendix has German-Boleshevik Conspiracy report.

Skousen, W. Cleon, *The Naked Communist,* Ensign Publications, 1958.
A textbook on Marxism-Leninism, the rise of the Communists to power and their activities since that time.

Sorokin, P. A., *Man and Society in Calamity,* E. P. Dutton & Co., New York, 1943.

Steffens, Lincoln, *The Autobiography of Lincoln Steffens,* New York, Harcourt, Brace & Co., 1931.
Radical pro-Communist Steffens accompanied Trotsky on his journey from New York to Russia.

Webster, Nesta, and Kerlan, Kurt, *Boche and Bolshevik*, New York, The Beckwith Co., 1923.
Discussion of role of Germany and international bankers in Bolshevik Revolution.

Willert, Arthur, *The Road to Safety*, London, Derek, Verschoyle, 1952.
Tells of Trotsky and Lenin's meeting, journey to Russia and how they were able to do so.

Zeman, Z. A. B. and Scharlau, W. B., *The Merchant of Revolution*, Oxford University Press, 1965.
Subtitled: The Life of Alexander Israel Helphand (Parvus). Contains information on German financing of Bolsheviks.

WORLD WAR I

Barnes, Harry Elmer, *Genesis of the World War*, New York, Alfred A. Knopf, 1927.
One of the original debunkings of the supposed causes of WWI.

dos Passos, John, *Mr. Wilson's War*, Garden City, N. Y., Doubleday, 1962.
Reveals Wilson's reluctance to hurt the Bolsheviks, much to the surprise of American Ambassador Francis.

Fay, Sidney B., *Origin Of The World War*, New York, Macmillan, 2 vols. in 1, 1931.
Basic revisionist textbook on WWI.

Foreign Relations of the United States, Paris Peace Conference, 1919, Vol. I and II, 1942, U. S. Government Printing Office.

Foreign Relations of the United States, The Lansing Papers 1914-1920, Vol. I, U. S. Government Printing Office, 1939.

George, Alexander and Juliette, *Woodrow Wilson and Colonel House*, New York, John Day, 1956.

My Memoirs: 1878-1918, Ex-Kaiser William II, London, New York, Toronto and Melbourne, Cassell and Company, Ltd., 1922.
Mentions that WWI had been planned for many years by European secret societies.

Lockhart, R. H. Bruce, *British Agent*, G. P. Putnam's Sons, New York and London 1933.

Neilson, Francis, *Makers of War*, Appleton, Wis., C. C. Nelson Co., 1950.
Discussion of the Sussex incident to draw America into the war.

Neilson, Francis, M. C., *How Diplomats Make War*, B. W. Huebsch, New York, 1916.

Ponsonby, Arthur, *Falsehood In War Time*, New York, E. P. Dutton & Co., Inc., 1928.
Delves into the cynicism of allied propaganda during WWI.

Strasser, Otto, *History In My Time*, London, Jonathan Cape, 1941.
Tells of groups behind the 1914 assassination of the Archduke Francis Ferdinand.

Tansill, Charles Callan, *America Goes To War*, Boston, Little, Brown, 1938.
Extremely thorough revisionist history of America's entrance into WWI.

Viereck, George Sylvester, *Spreading Germs of Hate*, New York, Horace Liveright, 1930.
Comparison of Allied and German war propaganda. Foreword written by Edward M. House, whose control over Wilson and guilt in helping to push America into WWI was to be exposed two years later in Viereck's *The Strangest Friendship in History*.

Von Clausewitz, Karl, *War, Politics, and Power,* Introduction by Edward M. Collins, A Gateway Edition, Henry Regnery, Chicago, 1962.

WORLD WAR II AND COMMUNISM

Barnes, Dr. Harry Elmer, *Perpetual War for Perpetual Peace,* Caxton Printers, Ltd., Caldwell, Idaho, 1953.

Beard, Charles A., *President Roosevelt and the Coming of the War,* 1941, Yale University Press, 1948.

Cooper, Duff, *The Second World War,* New York, Scribner's, 1939.
The view of one British *Insider* who, with Lord Halifax, had a great deal to do with bringing on the conflict he writes about.

Gisevius, Hans Bernd, *To The Bitter End,* Boston, Houghton Mifflin, 1947.
Especially interesting in connection with Reds in top Nazi circles.

Halifax, Lord, *American Speeches,* New York, Oxford University Press, 1947.
Some of these speeches are most interesting as to what this *Insider* was promoting.

Martin, James, *All Honorable Men,* New York, Little, Brown & Co., 1950.
Excellent on the behind-the-scenes maneuvering of international financiers in promoting WWII and taking advantage of its aftermath.

Neilson, Francis, *The Makers of War,* Appleton, Wis., C. C. Nelson Co., 1950.
Very valuable book on the machinations of the *Insiders* in America and England.

Nyomarkay, Joseph, *Charisma and Factionalism in the Nazi Party,* Minneapolis, Univ. of Minn. Press, 1967.
Good on Communists in the formation of and later in the Nazi movement.

Possony, Stefan T., *A Century of Conflict,* Chicago, Regnery, 1953.
See chapters on "The German-Bolshevik Conspiracy" and "Midwives of the Nazi Reich."

Reed, Douglas, *Nemesis: The Story of Otto Strasser And The Black Front,* New York, Boston, Houghton Mifflin, 1940.
Shows Marxian orientation of portion of Nazi leadership.

Sanborn, Frederic R., *Design For War,* New York, Devin-Adair, 1951.
Excellent on the causes of WWII.

Sasuly, Richard, *I. G. Farben,* New York, Boni & Gaer, 1947.
The story of the German Chemical empire that helped so mightily in Hitler's rise to total power in Germany, and whose legal problems were handled by Allen Dulles' law firm.

Strasser, Otto, *Hitler And I,* Boston, Houghton Mifflin Co., 1940.
Background on Hitler and his movement from one-time colleague.

Sturdza, Prince Michel, *The Suicide of Europe,* Boston and Los Angeles, Western Islands, 1968.
The former Foreign Minister of Rumania discusses the role of the Insiders in European politics prior to the beginning of WWI until the end of WWII.

Taylor, A. J. P., *Origins Of The Second World War,* London, Hamish Hamilton, 1961.
One of the few thorough revisionist studies of the causes of WWII.

Thyssen, Fritz, *I Paid Hitler,* New York, Farrar & Rinehart, 1941.
A top German industrialist who became disillusioned with Hitler and fled the Third Reich, reveals the role played by bankers and industrialists in Adolph

Hitler's rise to power.

Valtin, Jan, *Out Of The Night*, New York, Alliance, 1941.
How the Reds put the Nazis in power in Germany.

THE COUNCIL ON FOREIGN RELATIONS and THE ESTABLISHMENT

Allen, Gary, *Richard Nixon—The Man Behind the Mask*, Boston and Los Angeles, Western Islands, 1971.
In-depth study of the rise and reign of Richard Nixon; covers his relationship with the Rockefellers.

Barron, Bryton, *The Untouchable State Department*, Springfield, Va., Crestwood, 1962.
An inside view of the CFR-controlled State Department.

Browder, Earl, *Victory—And After*, New York, International, 1942.
The Communist position for the United Nations.

Carter, John Franklin, *Our Lords and Masters*, by the Unofficial Observer, Simon and Shuster, New York, 1935.

Carter, John Franklin, *The New Dealers*, by the Unofficial Observer, The Literary Guild, New York, 1934.

Cerf, Jay H. and Pozen, Walter [Editors], *Strategy For the 60's*, New York, Frederick A. Praeger, 1961.
Contains the CFR Study No. 7, advocating World Government.

Dall, Curtis, *F.D.R.—My Exploited Father-In-Law*, Tulsa, Christian Crusade Publications, 1968.
Intriguing personal account of the world of high finance and super-politics.

Domhoff, William G., *Who Rules America*, Prentice-Hall, Inc. New Jersey, 1967.

Flynn, John T., *Men of Wealth*, New York, Simon and Schuster, 1941.
Contains capsule biographies of several *Insiders* of the past.

Gannon, Francis X., *Biographical Dictionary Of The Left*, Vols. I and II, Boston, Western Islands, 1971.
Excellent short biographical sketches on many *Insiders*.

Hamill, John, *The Strange Career of Mr. Hoover Under Two Flags*, New York, William Faro, Inc., 1931.
Details Mr. Hoover's life as an errand boy for *Insiders*.

Hoffman, William, *David: Report On A Rockefeller*, New York, Lyle Stuart, 1971.
Despite rabid Leftist bias, this is an excellent research piece on the power of Rockefellers, Standard Oil and the Chase Manhattan Bank.

Johnson, Gerald W., *An Honorable Titan*, A biographical study of Adolph S. Oches, Harper & Brother Publishers, New York, 1946.

Jordan, Major George Racey, *From Major Jordan's Diaries*, Boston, Western Islands, 1965.
The incredible story of the transfer of American technology, patents and materials to Soviets during WWII.

Kunen, James, *The Strawberry Statement: Notes of a College Revolutionary*, New York, Random House.
Reveals how the super-rich from above are interested in financing street revolutionaries.

Lundberg, Ferdinand, *The Rich and the Super-Rich*, New York, Lyle Stuart, 1968.
While Mr. Lundberg does not understand that socialism is the tool of the

super-rich, his research provides a good deal of valuable information.

Lyons, Eugene, *The Red Decade*, Indianapolis, Bobbs-Merrill, 1941.
Contains information on pro-Communist bias of the *New Republic* which Quigley reveals was financed by Standard Oil heirs.

Martin, James J., *Revisionist Viewpoints*, Colorado Springs, Colo., 1971.
Covers aspects of WWII and Cold War. Quotes John Maynard Keynes concerning fact his system works best under a dictatorship.

McFadden, Louis T., *Collective Speeches of Congressman McFadden*, Hawthorne, Calif., Omni Publications, 1970.
A gold mine of information on international financiers from the former Chairman of the House Banking Committee.

Millin, Sarah Gertrude, *Cecil Rhodes*, Harper & Brothers, New York and London, 1933.

Neumann, Robert, *Zaharoff*, Alfred A. Knopf, New York, 1935.

Schlafly, Phyllis, *A Choice Not An Echo*, Alton, Ill., Pere Marquette Press, 1963.
Provides information on CFR-*Insider* control of the Republican Party at the top.

Shepardson, Whitney H., *Early History of the C.F.R.*, Stamford, Conn., The Overbrook Press, 1960.
A privately printed, limited edition account of the founding of the Council on Foreign Relations which mentions the role prominently played by Col. House, Paul Warburg and other *Insiders*.

Smith, Arthur D. Howden, *Men Who Run America*, Bobbs Merrill, 1935.

Smoot, Dan, *The Invisible Government*, The Dan Smoot Report, Inc. Dallas, 1962.

Stang, Alan, *The Actor*, Boston and Los Angeles, Western Islands, 1968.
John Foster Dulles and his brother Allen were key *Insiders* over a period of nearly four decades. An important book on the conspiracy.

Stettinius, Secretary of State Edward R., *State Department Publication 2349*.
Report to the President on the Results of the San Francisco Conference.

Sutton, Antony C., *Western Technology and Soviet Economic Development*, Volumes I and II, Hoover Institution, Stanford, 1968.

Webster, Nesta, *The Surrender of an Empire*, London, Boswell, Ltd., 1931.
Covers WWI, Bolsheviks and work of Royal Institute of International Affairs to dissolve British Empire.

White, Theodore, *The Making Of The President, 1960*, New York, Atheneum Publishers.
Provides information on Nixon's surrender to Rockefeller prior to the 1960 campaign.

Winkler, John K., *Morgan the Magnificent, The Life of J. Pierpont Morgan*, Doubleday, Doran & Co., Inc., Garden City, New York, 1932.

Winkler, John K., *John D.—A Portrait in Oils*, The Vanguard Press, New York, 1920.

Wormser, Rene, *Foundations: Their Power and Influence*, New York, Devin-Adair, 1958.
Provides a wealth of information concerning the activities of the Rockefeller and Carnegie Foundations.

CHAPTER FOOTNOTES

CHAPTER II

See John Robison's *Proofs of a Conspiracy*, Western Islands, Boston; Robert Payne's *Marx*, Simon & Schuster, New York, 1968, p. 30n.

CHAPTER III

①Remarks of Congressman John Rarick in the House of Representatives. *Congressional Record*, February 18, 1971.

②Emden, Paul H., *Money Powers of Europe*, D. Appleton, Century Company, 1938; Eaton, Clement, *History of the Southern Confederacy*, MacMillan, 1954.

③*National Economy And The Banking System*, Senate Documents, Volume 3, Number 23, 76th Congress, 1st Session, 1939.

④Marx, Karl, *The Communist Manifesto*, Henry Regnery Co., Chicago, 1954, p. 55.

⑤"Jew Baiting On The Left," *Jewish Frontier*, May 1940.

⑥*The Writings of Thomas Jefferson*, Vol. X, G. P. Putnam & Sons, New York, 1899, p. 31.

⑦Myers, Gustavus, *History of the Great American Fortunes*, Random House, New York, 1936, p. 556n.

⑧Hansl, Proctor, *Years of Plunder*, Harrison Smith & Robert Haas, New York, 1935, p. 90.

⑨*House Banking And Currency Committee Hearing* on H. R. 7230, 75th Congress, March 2 and 19, 1938, p. 214.

⑩Vanderlip, Frank, "Farm Boy to Financier, *Saturday Evening Post*, February 9, 1935, p. 25.

⑪Viereck, George S., *The Strangest Friendship in History*, Liveright, New York, 1932.

⑫Vanderlip, op. cit., p. 72.

⑬*Congressional Record*, December 22, 1913.

⑭Patman, Congressman Wright, Newsletter, June 6, 1968.

⑮Lindbergh, Charles A. Sr., *The Economic Pinch* [reprinted by Omni Publications, Hawthorne, Calif. 1968, p. 95.]

⑯Rothbard, Murray, *America's Great Depression*, Nash Publishing, Los Angeles, 1972, p. 86.

⑰Lundberg, Ferdinand, *America's 60 Families*, Vanguard Press, New York, 1938, p. 22.

⑱Bryan, Willian "John," *The United States Unresolved Monetary And Political Problems.* [Privately published]

⑲McFadden, Congressman Louis T., *On The Federal Reserve Corporation*, remarks in Congress, 1934, Forum Publication Co., Boston, p. 89.

⑳Hargrave, John, *Montagu Norman*, Greystone Press, New York, 1942.

CHAPTER IV

①Kolko, Gabriel, *The Triumph of Conservatism*, Quadrangle Books, Chicago, 1967, p. 4.

CHAPTER FOOTNOTES

②Lundberg, Ferdinand, *The Rich and The Super-Rich*, Lyle Stuart, Inc., New York, 1968, p. 350.

③Hinton, Harold Boaz, *Cordell Hull*, Garden City, New York, Doubleday Doran & Co., Inc., 1942.

④Ponsonby, Arthur, *Falsehood In War Time*, New York, E. P. Dutton & Co. Inc., 1928, p. 19.

⑤Dall, Curtis, *F.D.R.-My Exploited Father In Law*, Christian Crusade Publications, 1968, Tulsa, Okla., p. 71.

⑥Martin, Rose L., *The Fabian Freeway*, Western Islands, 1966, p. 163.

⑦Kennan, George F., *Russia and the West Under Lenin and Stalin*, Little, Brown & Co., 1960-61, p. 11.

⑧Shub, David, *Lenin*, Penguin Books, Baltimore, Md., 1967, pp. 201-206.

⑨Skousen, W. Cleon, *The Naked Communist*, Ensign Publications, 1958, pp. 110-115.

⑩Shub, op. cit., pp. 178-181, 205.

⑪Zeman, Z.A.B. and Scharlau, W. B., *Merchants of Revolution*, Oxford University Press, 1965, pp. 229-231.

⑫Willert, Arthur, *The Road To Safety*, London, Derek, Verschoyle, 1952, p. 29.

⑬Skousen, op. cit., p. 114.

⑭Shub, op. cit., p. 212.

⑮De Goulevitch, *Czarism and the Revolution* [translated from the original French publication by N. J. Couriss and reprinted by Omni Publications, Hawthorne, Calif., 1961], pp. 223-225, 231-232.

⑯Forbes, B. C., *Men Who Are Making America*, pp. 334-5.

⑰De Goulevitch, op. cit., p. 225.

⑱Hagedorn, Herman, *The Magnate*, John Day, N. Y. See also *Washington Post*, Feb. 2, 1918, p. 195.

⑲De Goulevitch, op. cit., p. 230.

⑳The leader of President Wilson's U. S. Commission to Revolutionary Russia was the so-called "Republican elder statesman" Elihu Root, who was formerly Secretary of State and War and was also the first honorary president and original founder of the CFR. See *CFR Annual Report*, June 30, 1969, and *Tragedy and Hope*.

㉑See testimony of former NKVD agent Peter Deriabin before the Senate Internal Security Subcommittee, March 26, 1965, in document "Murder and Kidnapping as an Instrument of Soviet Policy."

㉒The best general reference covering other areas of the conspiracy is Rose Martin's *Fabian Freeway*.

CHAPTER V

①House, Edward Mandell, *Philip Dru: Administrator: A Story Of Tomorrow, 1920-1935*, New York, B. W. Huebsch, 1920, p. 45.
②Millin, Sarah Gertrude, *Cecil Rhodes*, New York, Grossett & Dunlap, p. 98.

CHAPTER FOOTNOTES

③Quigley, Carroll, *Tragedy and Hope*, MacMillan, New York, 1966, p. 130.

④Aydelotte, Frank, *The American Rhodes Scholarships*, Princeton University Press, 1946, pp. 7-8.

⑤Quigley, op. cit., pp. 951-2.

⑥Quigley, op. cit., pp. 529–533.

⑦Cerf, Jay H., and Pozen, Walter [editors], *Strategy For the 60's*, Frederick A. Praeger, New York, 1961, p. 95.

⑧(Taken from C.F.R. membership roster and cross-referenced from Who's Who.)

⑨Quigley, op. cit., p. 950.

⑩Hatch, Alden, *Bernhard—Prince of the Netherlands*, New York, Doubleday & Co., 1962.

CHAPTER VI

①Louis Budenz, *The Bolshevik Invasion Of The West*, Bookmailer, p. 115.

②Antony Sutton, *Western Technology and Soviet Economic Development, 1917-1930, Hoover Institution on War, Revolution and Peace*, Stanford University, Calif. 1968, p. 292.

③O'Connor, Harvey, *The Empire of Oil*, Monthly Review Press, New York, 1955, p. 270.

④Ibid, Vol. I, p. 38.

⑤*National Republic*, Sept. 1927.

⑥Sutton, op. cit., Vol. II, p. 17.

⑦Ibid, Vol. II, p. 288.

⑧Ibid, Vol. II, p. 226.

⑨Ibid, p. 277.

⑩Ibid, Vol. II, p. 291.

⑪Congressional Record, June 15, 1933.

⑫See U. S. State Dept. Decimal File, 811.51/3711 and 861.50 "FIVE YEAR PLAN/236." Sutton, op. cit., Vol. II, p. 340n.

⑬Sutton, op. cit., Vol. II, p. 3.

CHAPTER VII

①Republican *Battle Line*, February 1970.

②*Newsweek*, January 11, 1971.

③Ibid.

④From a Nixon speech in Cleveland, Ohio in January 1968.

⑤Republican *Battle Line*, August 1969.

⑥(3) *Houston Tribune*, March 11, 1971.

⑦(Copy in possession of authors)

⑧Kunen, James, *The Strawberry Statement: Notes of a College Revolutionary*, Random House, New York, pp. 116-117.

⑨(*Human Events*, July 10, 1971.)

CHAPTER VIII

①Public Law 91-508, 91st Congress, H.R. 15073, October 26, 1970. An Act to amend the Federal Deposit Insurance Act to require insured banks to maintain certain records, to require that certain transactions in U. S. currency be reported to the Dept. of the Treasury, and for other purposes.

INDEX

195

For your reading pleasure ...